Towards a Spectral Microtonal Composition
A Bridge Between Arabic and Western Music

Towards a Spectral Microtonal Composition: A Bridge Between Arabic and Western Music

by

Rami Chahin

This book is written as a dissertation for the degree of PhD at Carl von Ossietzky University "Oldenburg University"

Bibliografische Information der Deutschen Nationalbibliothek

Die Deutsche Nationalbibliothek verzeichnet diese Publikation in der Deutschen Nationalbibliografie; detaillierte bibliografische Daten sind im Internet über http://dnb.d-nb.de abrufbar.

978-3-95983-092-8 (Paperback)

978-3-95983-093-5 (Hardcover)

© 2017 Schott Music GmbH & Co. KG, Mainz

Alle Rechte vorbehalten.
Nachdruck in jeder Form sowie die Wiedergabe durch Fernsehen, Rundfunk, Film, Bild- und Tonträger oder Benutzung für Vorträge, auch auszugsweise, nur mit Genehmigung des Verlags.

Printed in Germany

Preface

This work was originally written as a dissertation at Carl von Ossietzky University, where it was supervised by Prof. Violeta Dinescu and Prof. Dr. Joachim Dorfmüller. Their advice was very important in helping me to promote my work to achieve success in musicology, composition and theory.

Although the theoretical part was written as a harmonic solution for *maqam* music, it can be used as a universal function to develop theories in harmony in another traditional microtonal music.

This is one of the first idea dissertations in Germany based on the three musical fields of musicology, composition, and music theory. It needed much work, and here I would like to thank Prof. Dr. Wolfgang Stroh, Prof. Dr. Nicolae Manolache and Prof. Dr. Susanne Binas-Preisendörfer who were always ready to cooperate and react to my musical and scientific issues. Many also thanks go to the Syrian Ministry of Higher Education for supporting me with the scholarship I held from 2008 till 2011. Many thanks also go to Friedrich-Ebert-Stiftung for their scholarship which I held from 2012 until this work was complete. Further thanks and respect go to Friedrich-Ebert-Stiftung for sponsoring the printing of this book, and for their financial and incorporeal support.

Writing the opera *Qadmoos* in German took a lot of effort in translating the libretto from English into German. Here I would like to thank Ms. Carolyn Kurzhals, Mr. Gerhard Kurzhals, and Mr. Peter Haffmans for assisting with this.

The microtonal compositions I have written needed a lot of hard work and patience. I would like to thank the great musicians who voluntarily participated in bringing the work to success, Stefanie Golisch and Graham Waterhouse offered great encouragement, for which I thank them.

And finally, I would like to give my family and friends all the thanks for their moral support.

R. Chahin

Oldenburg

June 2017

Contents

1 Introduction	1
2 Questions and hypothesis	2
3 Background and literature	4
3.1 Theoretical background	4
3.1.1 Terminology	4
3.1.2 Worldwide tuning systems	7
3.1.3 Worldwide microtonality	14
3.1.4 Western microtonal music in the 20th century	16
3.2 Spectral- and overtone-music	18
3.2.1 Spectral music	18
3.2.2 Overtone music in western avant-garde	21
3.3 Fusions of Western and Arabic music	21
4 Performing practice of microtonal music	23
4.1 From 24-TET to 240-TET	23
4.2 Properties of the overtone series	26
5 A theory of spectral music	31
5.1 Overtone music in practice	31
5.1.1 The relationship of the overtones resultant from tones when they are played simultaneously or successively	32
5.1.2 The microtonal overtone scale (M.O.S.)	36
5.1.3 The chromatic microtonal overtone scale (C.M.O.S.)	37
5.1.4 The main overtone series, derived fundamental tone and the branch overtone series	39
5.2 The relationship between two or more tones from the first 16 overtones of the harmonic series	44
5.2.1 Fundamental tones in unison in horizontal movement	44
5.2.2 Fundamental tones in unison in vertical movement	44
5.2.3 The relationship between the fundamental tone and the overtones between the third and the sixteenth overtones	47
5.3 The relationship between the overtones and the common frequencies in regard to the fundamental tone	55

5.4 The microtonal harmony within the same harmonic series   57
5.4.1 The harmonies between two tones   57
5.4.2 The harmonies of three tones   62
5.4.3 The harmonic movement of three tones in microtonal overtone scale towards stability   66
5.4.4 The harmony of more than three tones   68
5.5 The modulation in the microtonal overtone tuning system   72
5.6 Linking overtones   75

6 The *maqam* system and the overtone series   78

6.1 Microtonality in Arabic Music   78
6.2 The properties of the *maqam*   81
6.3 The *maqamat* in a tuning-system of a harmonic series   85
6.4 The possible *ajnas* of the *maqamat* in the first four octaves of an overtone   87
6.5 The possible *ajnas* of the *maqamat* in the chromatic microtonal overtone scale   91
6.6 The overtone *maqam* in practice and modulation: The "Go in between system"   92

7 Musical instruments and special microtonal music   103

8 Analysis of my compositions in relation to the theory of spectral microtonal harmony   104

8.1 *Minus One Beautiful One* for cello   104
8.2 *Sudoku* for cello   106
8.3 *Sparkling Stone* for solo five- string cello   110
8.4 *Barada* for chamber ensemble   112
8.5 *Mesopotamian Tears* for woodwinds   115
8.6 Computer music for random microtonal overtone scales   118
8.7 Opera *Qadmoos*   120
8.7.1 Overture analysis   123
8.7.2 *Antara*   124

9 Conclusion   138

10 Perspective of the theory   140

Bibliography 141

Tables 147

Figures 147

Samples from Opera *Qadmoos*, *Storyteller* scene *"Antara"* 154

1 Introduction

The music of the Arabic world and the music of the Western world are different because they are the outcomes of different cultures on different continents. Throughout history, bridges have been established to link the creation of music of both cultures. Exchanges in musical composition have been set in motion by both sides, reflecting an interchange of elements from east and west. Elements of the music of the Babylonians,[1] the Phoenicians, and the Egyptians,[2] can be traced to the music of the Greeks, Romans, Byzantines and the Islamic era.[3] Intertextuality arising from the mutual exchange in musical theories has enabled the appearance of new international tuning systems.

In this book the theory of composing Spectral Microtonal Music and other examples of my own compositions based on this theory are expounded. This work is presented as musicological research illustrated by related compositions. I will first consider the historical background of Arabic and Western music and then will demonstrate how, according to this theory, some essential features of Western spectral music of the twentieth century can be combined with the specific microtonality of traditional and new Arabic music, thus forming a new transcultural link between two important cultures.

The theory of Spectral Microtonal Music is considered a complex phenomenon as demonstrated by:

1) Historical references

2) Basic facts of acoustics

3) Previous experiences of other microtonal and spectral composers

4) Various compositions I have written including the opera *Qadmoos,* on which this book is based.

Writing this musicological work for a practical demonstration faced many difficulties, especially as the research deals with two components at the same time: Arabic traditional music (*Maqam* music) and contemporary European music composition (spectral music). The composition of the opera *Qadmoos* thereby leads to the tangible proof of the thesis through the implementation of the theoretical research of *Spectral Microtonal Music*.

---

[1] McClain, Ernest G. *The Pythagorean Plato.* York Beach 1984, p.3.
[2] Williams, Abdy C.F. *The Aristoxenian Theory of Musical Rhythm.* Cambridge UP, Cambridge 2009, p.9.
[3] Mitchell, Terence. *Another Look at Alleged Ancient Bagpipes.* In *Proceedings of the International Conference of Near Eastern Archaeomusicology ICONEA 2008.* Richard Drumbill & Irving Finkel, eds. Lulu, London 2010, p.38.

2 Questions and hypothesis

The purpose of the research is attempt to redefine world music through the use of a musical technique by which elements of Western music and Arabic music merge, resulting in a new method of spectral microtonal music that echoes aspects of both Eastern and Western cultures.

The aesthetic background of this book is based on compositions that form the practical part of the work. The different methods used in the compositions facilitate the understanding of the theory. Spectral music was discovered by composers at the end of the twentieth century. It was based on the acoustic property of the sound, so harmonics play a significant role. *Maqam*[4] music is based on early theories and tuning systems from the Islamic era, between the eighth and fourteenth centuries. The compositional theories that depend on overtones are mainly based on spectral and *maqam* music.

Spectral technique and microtonal *maqam* technique are the two musical devices used in the composition of *Qadmoos*. Consequently, I argue that Western and Arabic music can be merged or fused through the use of the overtone series or the musical spectrum. The tuning systems developed in the Islamic period originated in the musical theories of the Greek and Roman eras.

The theoretical part of this book, Chapters 5 and 6, along with the compositions aim to substantiate the following:
- The harmonic series has been used generally to legitimatize Western tone-systems: the hierarchy of consonance/dissonance, the rules of tonal composition with diatonic harmonies, and the expansion of the tonal system into atonality or augmentative tonality (Schönberg's *Harmonielehre*, Hindemith's *Unterweisung im Tonsatz*) along with some microtonal systems in the twentieth century.
- The overtone series can be used to explain the microtonal practice within Arabic music.[5] Similarly, the main theories in Arabic music,[6] which were de-

---

[4] "The term for 'mode' used by practising musicians in the Middle East is *naghm* (pl. *angham*). However, the term *maqam*, retained by the Turks among others, was also used by theorists at the beginning of the 20th century. It asserted itself as standard terminology through the agency of Western musicology, which sanctioned it and devoted much attention to it." Poché, Christian: *Arab music., The New Grove Dictionary of Music and Musicians*, 2nd ed., vol.1, Macmillan Publishers Limited, London 2001, p.813.

[5] Habib Touma's work is based on the work of the philosopher Al-Farabi who lived from 872-950: الفارابى Al-Farabi, Abu Nasr كتاب الموسيقى الكبير / *Kitab Al-Musiqa Al-Kabir*/ *The Great Book of Music* : Egyptian National Library and Archives, Cairo 2009; Touma, Habib H. *The Music of the Arab*. Cambridge UP, Cambridge 2003, pp.17–24.

[6] The main theoretical contributions in tuning systems written between the nineteenth and thirteenth centuries were written by Al-Kindi, Al-Farabi, Al-Urmawi.

veloped between the nineteenth and thirteenth centuries,[7] were based on the ratios of the overtone series. The deviations of the pitches in a *maqam* from the simple diatonic scale are derived from the overtones 4 to 6: f-a-c, c-e-g, g-h-d[8] as three pure triads, or the tempered diatonic scale consisting of intervals 2-2-1-2-2-2-1 of the equal-twelve-temperament.[9]

- Western spectral music and overtone music, music based on overtones such as Tuvan throat singing in Mongolia, show that the traditional equal-tempered chromatic tuning and the tonal systems based on it can be further developed and augmented by using intervals between overtones which have not been used in Western music: the intervals in the overtone series 7-8, 10-11, 11-12, 12-13, 13-14, 14-15, 20-21. This phenomenon can be considered as the meeting point between Arab music and Western music.

- The advanced microtonal music in the sense of the meeting point reveals certain practical problems which have to be solved if a theory of spectral microtonal music is to be established. Examples of such practical problems may be: the coincidence of the spectrum of each tone with a chord or melody, and the spectral structure of harmonic or melodic flow based mainly on the overtones of the spectrum. Further issues to consider relate to which instruments may be suitable for such music, and what skills are required for musicians to perform it.

- The last and possibly the most important question is whether this theory of spectral music can be applied in composition.

---

[7] Maalouf, Shireen. *History of Arabic Music Theory*. Kaslik, Lebanon 2002.
[8] I use the German style for writing accidentals, where H is equal to B in English.
[9] Loy, Gareth R. *Musimathics, The Mathematical Foundations of Music*. vol.1, MIT Press, Cambridge 2006, pp.39–40.

3 Background and literature

3.1 Theoretical background

3.1.1 Terminology

Here I define the most important terminology to be found in this work, with reference to a commentary by the musicologist C.M. Atkinson, who attests that "tone system or scale, mode or tone, and musical notation, obviously, each of these topics is vast in its own right, each has been investigated extensively, and each still deserves further studies of its own." [10] The stipulations of musical languages are in a state of continuous change; consequently the terms connected to them are continuously reinterpreted and changed. These changes have historical as well as cultural reasons and have led to a situation in which some terms appear with different definitions. It is then necessary to redefine certain music-theoretical terms in order to be applicable to my theory and the related compositions.

Tuning system:

The term tuning system (or tone system) describes the conjunction of pitches, i.e. their different configuration in form of tone scales as well as the relationship between different tones of the tone scale. Different tuning systems may share a common tuning system. [11] The definition of tuning systems depends on historical and cultural factors which have influenced the characteristics of different tone systems.

There are varieties of tuning systems related to different traditions and cultures. We find different tuning systems within a single country or within small regions, however, in some areas, we do not find many tuning systems at all. Sometimes we find similarities in tuning systems within certain cultures; this similarity can also be found in cultures that have nothing in common and no close geographic connections. Obvious similarities can be traced in the tuning systems of the music of some cultures in Asia, the Middle East, Africa and Europe. This similarity is related to the basic hypothesis that some researchers have used in their tuning systems; for example most of the old cultures like the Sumerians, Egyptians, Chinese, and the Greeks used the cycle of fifths as a hypothesis. Theories based on the cycle of fifths or fourths are the most

---

[10] Atkinson, Charles M. *The Critical Nexus Tone-System, Mode, and Notation in Early Medieval Music.* Oxford UP, Oxford 2009, p.4.

[11] Sometimes in the main tuning system, there are different ways of tunings, which I call branch tuning systems. For example, the tuning system of Arabic, Persian, and Turkish music is the *maqam* with different intervals in the *maqamat* of each culture.

common. The cycle of fifths or fourths three-limit[12] played a significant role in ancient musical mythology.[13] The most important civilizations which implemented these theories were the Mesopotamian in the third millennium B.C.,[14] the ancient Egyptian, the ancient Greek, the ancient Indian, and the ancient Chinese.

Aspects of early theories of tuning systems still resonate and have points in common; but at the same time each of these civilizations maintains its character while employing its own tuning system and its own instrumentation. This characteristic is the mode of their tuning system.

Although the above-mentioned civilizations used similar mathematical background theories, their modes differ. For example, we can find similar modes to the Western major, minor, pentatonic in the *raga* system, *dastgah* system, *lü* system[15] and the *maqam* system.

In the compositions related to the theory in spectral and microtonal music in Chapter 5 and 6, different tone systems are used not only consecutively, but also simultaneously. This is a result of the dramatic concept of the libretto of the opera *Qadmoos*, which directly influences the nature of the musical language. Therefore, as an extension of the term tone system, the term multitone system is used.

Overtones, Spectrum:

Any tone from a musical instrument is made up of waves of various different frequencies. These frequencies are numerically related to the first frequency, or fundamental tone, and in theory they continue infinitely:

> "[C]omplex sound waves can be decomposed into a family of simple sine waves, each of which is characterized by its frequency, amplitude, and phase. These are called the partials, or the overtones of the sound, and the collection of all the partials is called the spectrum."[16]

The spectrum shows the energy distribution of a waveform as an assembly of frequencies.[17] My research encompasses a range of about 200 overtones. From this overall range I select certain overtones which are assembled in relation to different musical and textual contexts.

---

[12] Limit was first used by Harry Partch. This term describes the greatest prime number of an overtone rational number in a tuning system. Partch has used it to compare his 11-limit tuning system with the 3-limit Pythagorean system.
[13] Almost all ancient music theory was based on mythology and the perfection of the number twelve.
[14] McClain, Ernest. *A Sumerian Text in Quantified Archaeomusicology*. In *Proceedings of the International Conference of Near Eastern Archaeomusicology ICONEA 2008*, Richard Drumbrill & Irving Finkel, eds. Lulu, London 2010, p.89.
[15] Daniélou, Alain. *Music and The Power of Sound*. Inner Traditions, Rochester 1995, p.39.
[16] Sethares, William A. *Tuning, Timbre, Spectrum, Scale*. 2nd ed. London, London 2005, p.13.
[17] Loy 2006, p.30.

Spectral music:

Music by nature has a spectral aspect; however, it was in 1970s that European composers began to explicitly concentrate on acoustic characteristics of sound spectra.[18] They used sound spectra as a source of inspiration in the process of determining their musical material.

The term "spectral music" first appeared in Hugues Dufort's 1979 article *Musique spectral,*[19] written before the spectral movement was established.[20]

In addition to acoustic music, electronic music and computer music are essential aspects of the field of spectral music.[21]

Microtone, Microintervalls, Microtonality:

A microtone can be defined as:

> "Any musical interval or difference of pitch distinctly smaller than a semitone. Some writers restrict the term to quantities of less than half a semitone; others extend it to refer to all music with intervals markedly different from the (logarithmic) 12th part of the octave and its multiples, including such scales with fewer than 12 pitches as are used, for example, in south-east Asia."[22]

In the twentieth century the above mentioned terms were used in various ways; these are discussed in section 3.1.4.

Microtonality has always been possible; however, since Western Europe started to use the tempered system, microtones and micro-intervals have been ignored.[23] At the beginning of the twentieth century, composers found new ways of integrating microtones and micro-intervals into new tonalities, from which microtonality emerged, using different tone systems from the tempered scale.[24]

A significant aspect of my work is based on the 72-TET,[25] in which an octave is divided into 72 pitches and the 24-TET which is used in traditional Arabic music. They are used instead of the common 12- TET. These tone systems are assimilated to the overtone series by fixing the pitches of the overtones in relation to the nearest equivalent pitch belonging to the 72-TET or 24-TET.

---

[18] Anderson, Julian. *Spectral music.*, The New Grove Dictionary of Music and Musicians. 2nd ed., vol.24, Macmillan Publishers Limited, London 2001, p.166.
[19] Dufourt, Hugues. *Musique spectral.* Société Nationale de Radiodiffusion,Radio-France, March 1979. Reprinted in *Conséquences* nos.7–8, Paris 1986, pp.111–115.
[20] I will go into details about this topic in section 3.3.
[21] Miranda, Eduardo Reck. *Computer Sound Design.* Focal Press, Oxford 2002, p. xvii.
[22] Griffiths, Paul, Mark Lindley, and Ioannis Zannos *Microtone.*, The New Grove Dictionary of Music and Musicians. 2nd ed., vol.16, Macmillan Publishers Limited, London 2001, p.624.
[23] Metzger, Heinz-Klaus & Riehn, Rainer. *Musik-Konzepte Sonderband Musik der anderen Tradition. Mikrotonale Tonwelten.* Richard Borrberg, München 2003, p.59.
[24] Composers such as Alois Haba, Charles Ives, Julian Carrillo, and George Enescu used microtonality.
[25] TET stands for tone equal temperament system, which means equal intervals between tones in the octave base on logarithms.

Microtonal Overtone Scale:

To distinguish between the term overtone scale[26] from the scale that is used in this theory, the adjective microtonal is added. The related scales for the term overtone scale in western 12-tone music are the Lydian Dominant scale[27] and acoustic scale.[28]

3.1.2 Worldwide tuning systems

> "In the literature on tuning systems, the arguments for and against the various tuning -systems sound as though they were referring to wine tasting."[29]

Tuning is the principal action a musician undertakes before any performance. Its importance varies, and depends on historical as well as cultural factors, for example the old Greek tuning systems are microtonal and vary and the new ones are performed within the tempered 12-tone system. The tuning systems can be classified into three main groups depending on the theory or idea behind each one. These groups are:

1) Tuning systems based on overtone ratios;
2) Equal temperament tuning systems, which have no microtonal differences between intervals;
3) Tuning systems which have neither physical nor mathematical reasons, but which owe their existence to logical or traditional factors, where musicians tune their instruments by ear.

The first two groups are divided into branch groups including the 12-tone tuning systems that have 12 intervals in an octave in a microtonal or a tempered scale. These branches are considered a xenharmonic tuning.[30]

The examples below for these three groups illustrate the classification of the microtonal overtone scale and the chromatic microtonal overtone scale discussed further in this work:

1) Tuning systems based on overtone ratios

A. Tuning systems based on overtone ratios of small whole numbers in the numerator and in the denominator. Examples of this kind of tuning are:

- *Just Intonation 12-tone tuning system*: these tunings are found on a pure major third (5:4), and are divided into two different major seconds 9:8 and 10:9.

---

[26] Persichetti, Vincent. *Twentieth-Century Harmony*. W.W.Norton & Company, New York 1961, p.44.
[27] I use a special microtonal notation, different from the overtone scale. This is used by many composers in a simple tempered form.
[28] Burt, Peter. *The Music of Toru Takemitsu*. Cambridge UP, Cambridge 2003, p.81.
[29] Loy 2006, p.69.
[30] A xenharmonic tuning refers to a tuning not possible in 12- TET. Sethares 2005, p.xviii.

For example:

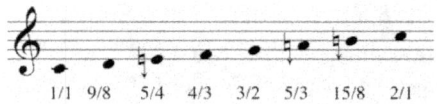

Figure 1: *Ptolemy's Syntonic Diatonic* Scale. [31]

- The Guqin[32] tuning: This Chinese instrument is tuned in the following ratios: (1/8, 1/6, 1/5, 1/4, 1/3, 2/5, 1/2, 3/5, 2/3, 3/4, 4/5, 5/6, 7/8, and 1/1).[33]
- Spectral Scales:[34] Two scales prove this theory. These scales are built on the successive tones on the fourth or the fifth octaves of the overtone series. The first scale starts on the eighth overtone and ends on the sixteenth overtone:

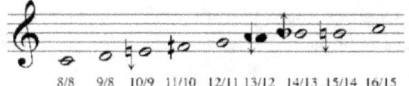

Figure 2: Scale from the harmonic series in the fourth octave. Each interval ratio is written in a relation to the previous tone.

The second scale starts on the sixteenth overtone and ends on the thirty-second overtone:

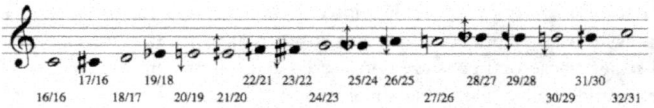

Figure 3: Scale from the harmonic series in the fifth octave. Each interval ratio is written in a relation to the previous tone.

Sethares, in his book *Tuning, Timbre, Spectrum, Scale* says:

> "Spectral scales, even more than JI, tend to be restricted to particular keys or tonal centers. They contain many of the just intervals when played in the key of the fundamental on which they are based, but the approximations become progressively worse in more distant keys."[35]

---

[31] Loy 2006, p.55.
[32] Guqin is a Chinese musical instrument also written Tjin.
[33] Reinhard, Kurt. *Chinesische Musik*. Erich Röth-Verlag, Kassel 1956, p.77.
[34] Sethares 2005, p.66.
[35] Sethares 2005, p.69.

Both scales are used on different occasions, and I call the first one the microtonal overtone-scale (M.O.S.) and the second one the chromatic microtonal overtone-scale (C.M.O.S.).

B. Tuning systems that have high numbers in the numerator and/or in the denominator of the fraction. In this classification, we find all the theories which are based on succession of certain ratio or scales which use high rational numbers in the numerator and/or in the denominator to complete an octave:
- The Pythagorean tuning system, the system of the cycle of fifths (3:2)[36] or three-limit: All previous tuning systems are based on theories that deal in pure fifths. Some of these theories can be traced back to the Babylonian era.[37] For example:

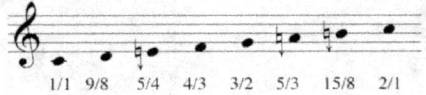

Figure 4: Pythagorean diatonic scale.

- Bohlen-Pierce Scale:[38] This is a non-octave scale.[39] It starts with a tone and ends with that tone's pure overtonal-fifth (3/1) (1200+702=1902cents). The idea of this scale comes from the overtones of woodwind instruments such as the pan flute and the clarinet, the spectrums of which have odd harmonics: 1*f*, 3*f*, 5*f*, 7*f*.[40] This scale is based on the triad ratios 3:5:7:[41]

---

[36] Benson, David J. *Music: A Mathematical Offering*. Cambridge UP, Cambridge 2008, p.211. *p-limit*: P (Prime number) is the highest number which the rational numbers in denominators and numerators factor can reach.
[37] McClain. *The Pythagorean Plato,* Nicolas-Hays, Inc., York Beach 1984, p.8 & 149.
See also: Crickmore, Leon. *New Light on the Babylonian Tonal System. Proceedings of the International Conference of Near Easten Archaeomusicology: held at the British Museum, December 4, 5 and 6, 2008, ICONEA, London 2010,* p.17; McClain, *The Myth Of Invariance.* Nicolas-Hays, Inc, 1984. p.133; Williams 2009, p.9.
[38] Walker, Elaine. *The Bohlen-Pierce Scale: Continuing Research.* Final Project in Advanced Acoustics, NYU, 2001. http://ziaspace.com/NYU/BP-Scale_research.pdf) Accessed. 7 Feb. 2016.
[39] A non-octave scale is a sequence of notes ascending or descending from a certain pitch, not in an octave. The non-octave scale starts and ends with different tones and an octave is not its limit.
[40] Sethares 2005, p.111.
[41] I am adding 9/1 in the example below as an answer to the ratio 3/1. The first scale is within the ratios 1/1 and 3/1, and the second scale is from 3/3 to 9/3. The ninth overtone is the perfect fifth for third overtone.

3	5	7	9	Overtone no.
3/3=1/1	3/5=>9/5	3/7=> 9/7	3/9	3
5/3	5/5=1/1	5/7=> 15/7	5/9=> 5/3	5
7/3	7/5	7/7=1/1	7/9=> 7/3	7
9/3= 3/1	9/5	9/7	9/9=1/1	9

Table 1: Way to have the main tones in *Bohlen-Pierce* Scale.[42]

From the previous table it can be concluded that the main tones are:

Ratios of tones	Interval ratios of tones
1/1	0
9/7	9/7
7/5	49/45
5/3	25/21
9/5	27/25
15/7	25/21
7/3	49/45
3/1	9/7

Ratios of tones	Interval ratios of tones	Intervals between tone (cent)
1/1	0	0
9/7	9/7	435
7/5	49/45	147
5/3	25/21	302
9/5	27/25	133
15/7	25/21	302
7/3	49/45	147
3/1	9/7	435

Table 2: Ratios of main tones in the *Bohlen–Pierce Scale*.

The smallest intervals among the previous tones are between 9/7 and 7/5, 5/3 and 9/5, and between 15/7 and 7/3; in cents it is 133 and 147. These intervals allow the scale to be divided into thirteen tones with almost equal intervals, on average 1902/13≈146.3cents per interval:

Tones n.	Interval ratios of tones to m in-tone	Intervals ratios in relation to previous t	Just tuning of the tones interval ratios to main-tone (cent)	Intervals in (cent)
1	1/1	0	0	0
2	27/25	27/25	133	33
3	25/21	625/567	302	169
4	9/7	27/25	435	133
5	7/5	49/45	583	147
6	75/49	375/343	737	154
7	5/3	49/45	884	147
8	9/5	27/25	1018	133
9	49/25	49/45	1165	147
10	15/7	375/343	1319	154
11	7/3	49/45	1467	147
12	63/25	27/25	1600	133
13	25/9	625/567	1769	169
14	3/1	27/25	1902	133

Table 3: Intervals in *Bohlen-Pierce Scale*[43].

---

[42] When a ratio is less than *Bohlen-Pierce's* octave, it will be multiplied by three to make it within an octave, for example 3/5 is less than (3*3)/7=9/7.

- Harry Partch's 43-tone Scale: This scale is based on the tuning system of 11-limit, referring to the highest overtone to which this system is limited. Other tones, even the ones which have higher overtones than 11, descend from the first 11 overtones. For instance, the basic overtones of the overtone 81/80 are 3/2 and 5/4: $81/80=(81/64)/(5/4)=(3/2)^4/(5/4)$.
In this tuning system the main pure intervals of the just intonation system are seen. For example, the octave 2/1, perfect fifth 3/2, major third 5/4, minor third 6/5, perfect fourth 4/4. These intervals are illustrated in the Partch 11-limit tonality diamond:

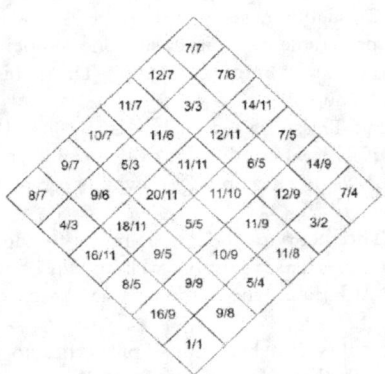

Tone no.	Interval	Interval (cent)	Tone no.	Interval	Interval (cent)	Tone no.	Interval	Interval (cent)
1	1/1	0	16	14/11	418	31	18/11	853
2	81/80	22	17	9/7	435	32	5/3	884
3	33/32	53	18	21/16	471	33	27/16	906
4	21/20	85	19	4/3	498	34	12/7	933
5	16/15	112	20	27/20	520	35	7/4	969
6	12/11	151	21	11/8	551	36	16/9	996
7	11/10	165	22	7/5	583	37	9/5	1018
8	10/9	182	23	10/7	618	38	20/11	1034
9	9/8	204	24	16/11	649	39	11/6	1049
10	8/7	231	25	40/27	681	40	15/8	1088
11	7/6	267	26	3/2	702	41	40/21	1116
12	32/27	294	27	32/21	729	42	64/33	1147
13	6/5	316	28	14/9	765	43	160/81	1179
14	11/9	347	29	11/7	783	1^	2/1	1200
15	5/4	386	30	8/5	814			

Table 4: Diamond and the 43-tone Scale of H.Partch.[44]

---

[43] Walker 2001, p.3. modified by R.Ch.
[44] Schuler, Thomas Herwig. *Mikrotonalität und ihre Wurzeln bei Harry Partch*. In *Musikzeit. Mikrotonal Komponieren*. Marion Diederichs-Lafite, ed., ÖMZ, Wien 2008, p.18.

C. Tuning systems are originally found in the Pythagorean theory of the cycle of pure fifths, which then developed into the tempered 12-tone system. The microtonal intervals are sometimes modified toward the temperament system as a way to fix the measurement of all intervals in an octave. At other times, the theorist tries to keep the pure intervals (mainly the pure fifth, third and the pure third) within their designated system:

- Mean tone temperament: This term was used in the eighteenth century to describe keyboard tunings from the fifteenth century to the eighteenth. These tunings are found by optimizing the pure major thirds (5:4) and also the pure fifth (3:2), slightly raised or lowered by ratios from the Pythagorean comma. The preferable ratios in mean tone temperament are the quarter-, fifth-, and the sixth-comma mean tone. These thirds are divided into two equal major seconds.[45]
- Well temperament: This term was first used by J. S. Bach in *Das wohltemperierte Clavier* in 1722,[46] where the aim of the tuning is to maintain equality between the intervals as far as possible, while keeping the intervals purely intoned.[47]
- *Maqam* System: The theory of the Arabic music tuning systems was developed by different theorists, the most well-known of whom are Al-Kindi, Al-Urmawi and Al-Farabi, whose theories are based on the Pythagorean theory.[48]
- The Persian tuning system has similar properties to the Arabic system; however three main theories in the field of Persian tuning systems were developed at the beginning of the twentieth century. The first theory was written by Ali Naqi Vaziri in 1920. His theory concludes that Persian music is based on 24-quarter ton scale.[49] The second theory was developed by Mehdi Barkesli in the 1940s. His theory concludes that Persian music is based on 22-quarter tone scale. The third theory was proposed by Hormoz Farhat in 1990. His theory is that the Persian tuning system, the *dastgah*, gives more flexibility and freedom for using the intervals.[50]

---

[45] Lindley, Mark. *Mean-tone*. The New Grove Dictionary of Music and Musicians. 2nd ed., vol.24, Macmillan Publishers Limited, London 2001.
[46] Cope, David. *Virtual Music*. MIT Press, Cambridge 2004, p.224.
[47] Loy 2006, p.69.
[48] In the theoretical part of Chapter 6 the practical part of the *maqam* music is classified in the third classification of tuning systems.
[49] Farhat, Hormoz. *The Dastgah Concept in Persian Music*. Cambridge UP, Cambridge 1990, p.9.
[50] Farhat 1990, p.7.

These three theories established new rules to define the intervals of the *maqamat*[51] in the Persian music. These new definitions for the intervals within the Person *maqamat* differ from the Arabic *maqam*.

2) Equal temperament tuning systems are based on a logarithmic interval means that the intervals have an equal ratio: of $y^{1/n} = a$.[52]

- 12-tone equal temperament tuning systems (12-TET): The intervals within an octave are divided equally in the ratio of $2^{1/12}$ for the interval which is equal to 100 cents. An octave has 1200 cents, thus each smaller interval is 1200/12=100 cents.
- 24-tone equal temperament tuning systems (24-TET): The intervals within an octave are divided equally in the ratio of $2^{1/24}$ which is equal to 50 cents as main and smaller intervals in the octave. This tuning system is used in some keyboard instruments, such as the Casio Oriental Keyboard AT-5 the and Korg Pa600 QT Oriental Entertainer Workstation
- 19-tone equal temperament tuning-systems (19-TET): in which an octave is divided into 19 equal intervals where each one is equal to $2^{1/19}$, or ~63.158 cents for the each interval in an octave.

In some cases, these two groups can be simulated treated similarly to each other when the difference in cents between the ratio interval and the logarithmic equal temperament intervals is not as large, for example, mean-tone temperament, well-temperament, the just intonation 12-tone tuning-system, the Ptolemy Diatonic Scale and *Maqam Hijaz*, which can be written in 12-TET.

3) Tuning systems that have no clear physical or mathematical background, but have a logical and/or traditional concept, can be found everywhere, even in nature. For example, the melodies sung by birds are songs inherited from their elders. The tones of the songs are related to special tuning systems suitable to their sound physiology.[53]

Tuning systems in traditional music are generally inherited from previous generations. This can help to explain the difference in intervals in a tuning system from a place to another in a given culture. For example, in Persian music the difference in performing the natural second and the natural third can reach 45 cents from one musician to another:[54]

---

[51] In Persian music the word *maye* is the synonym for the Arabic and Turkish tuning system *maqam*. *Maqamat*: Singular *maqam*, plural *maqamat*.
[52] Sethares 2005, p.59.
[53] Clark, Xenos. *The American Naturalist, Animal Music, its Nature and Origin*. Vol.xiii, The University of Chicago Press, Chicago 1879, p.15.
[54] Farhat 2004, p.26.

The natural second interval is between 125 cents and 170 cents.
The natural third is between 325 cents and 370 cents.
The intervals in the Arabic *maqam* music are similar to those in Persian *maqam*, but the intervals inside each *maqam* have different ratios from each others.[55] Different cultures in the same country or place can have completely different intervals in the same *maqam*.

3.1.3 Worldwide microtonality

Microtonal music is wide spread. The traditional music of Thailand is an example of microtonal music from Asia that can be different from one place to another, or even from one gamelan ensemble to another in the same city. Thai music and instruments were originally influenced by Chinese, Indonesian, Indian and indigenous Khmer music and instruments. It has two main scale systems: *pélog* and *sléndro*; however it is difficult to find two ensembles which have the same tuning. Margaret Kartomi writes that "Javanese tuners seek not to replicate pre-existing tunings, but to create for each ensemble a unique tuning that remains recognizably *sléndro* or *pélog* and pleasing."[56]

What follows are some examples of the two scales:

(1)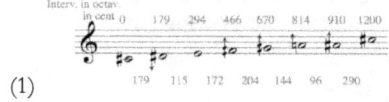

Figure 5: Balinese *pélog* (saih 7) Krobokan village

(2)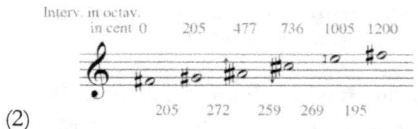

Figure 6: *Sléndro* scale from gender dasa, Kuta village

---

[55] Different cultures in the same country or place can have completely different intervals in the same *maqam*.
[56] Kartomi, Margaret, et al. *Indonesia*. in *The Garland Handbook of Southeast Asian Music*. Terry E. Miller& Sean Williams, eds. Routledge, London 2008, p.358.

Figure 7: Comparing *pélog* scale with *sléndro* scales[57]

Figure 8: *Sléndro* scale and *pélog* scale from Bali gamelan examples for *prélog* scale and one for *sléndro* scale[58]

As an example of microtonal music in India, we can consider *carnatic* music,[59] which is characteristic of southern India.[60] It is one of the major traditions of Indian classical music in additional to the *Hindustani* in northern India.[61] There are different elements in *carnatic* music like *raga, sruti*,[62] *swara, tala* and the *melakarta* systems which can be used to classify and understand south Indian *raga*. There are some similarities between *maqam* and *raga*. "[…] Amir Khusrau (1253–1325) is credited as the musician who incorporated Persian and Sanskrit, Islamic and Hindu *maqam* and raga with classical elements to form a new music."[63]

Sruti is the Indian counterpart to musical intervals used for in musical scales.[64] These musical scales are the most common Hindustani scales, and have 22 *srutis*[65] per octave:[66]

---

[57] For example, this method is used by composers when they want to compose a piece by using a *pélog* gamelan derived from *sléndro*.
[58] McPhee, Colin. *Music in Bali,* Da Capo Press, New York 1976, pp.40–52.
[59] Lahiri, Aditi. *The Grammar of Carnatic Music,* Walter de Gruyter GmbH & Co. KG, Berlin 2007.
[60] Krishnaraj, S. *Carnatic India: Carnatic Music History and Evolution*, 2006–15. http://www.carnaticindia.com/carnatic_music.html. Accessed 7 Feb. 2016.
[61] Nidel, Richard. *World Music: The Basics*. Routledge, London 2005, p.219.
[62] Sometimes this is also written *shrutis*.
[63] Nidel 2005, p.220.
[64] Loy 2006, p.79.
[65] Each *sruti* is approximately equal to a quartertone.
[66] McClain, Ernest G. *The Myth of Invariance*. Nicolas-Hays, Inc., York Beach 1984, p.38.

Degree	Ratio	Cents	Interval	Size
1	1/1	0	–	–
2	256/243	90.23	256/243	90.23
3	16/15	111.73	81/80	21.51
4	**10/9**	**182.40**	**25/24**	**70.67**
5	9/8	203.91	81/80	21.51
6	32/27	294.14	256/243	90.23
7	6/5	315.64	81/80	21.51
8	5/4	386.31	25/24	70.67
9	81/64	407.82	81/80	21.51
10	4/3	498.05	256/243	90.23
11	**27/20**	**519.55**	**81/80**	**21.51**
12	**45/32**	**590.22**	**25/24**	**70.67**
13	729/512	611.73	81/80	21.51
14	3/2	701.96	256/243	90.23
15	128/81	792.18	256/243	90.23
16	8/5	813.69	81/80	21.51
17	5/3	884.36	25/24	70.67
18	27/16	905.87	81/80	21.51
19	16/9	996.09	256/243	90.23
20	**9/5**	**1017.60**	**81/80**	**21.51**
21	15/8	1088.27	25/24	70.67
22	243/128	1109.78	81/80	21.51

Table 5: 22 *srutis* in the *Hindustani* scale.[67]

Africa is a rich continent with regard to the variety of tuning systems. North Africa is dominated by *maqam* music.

One of the instruments that performs on a fixed tuning-system in central Africa is the *Akogo* from Congo:[68]

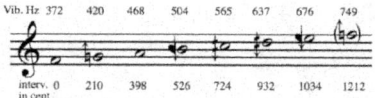

Figure 9: Intervals in an *Akogo*

3.1.4 Western microtonal music in the 20th century

Gareth Loy describes the first reaction of the Western musicians towards microtonal music as follows:

> "One of the main thrusts of early Western microtonal tunings was to increase the number of scale degrees on keyboards. The original aim was to supply alternative choices of intervals when modulating or transposing so as to retain as much as possible the simple integer ratios of the just scales. Such a scale system would then contain microtones, which are scale degrees that are smaller than a semitone."[69]

---

[67] Daniélou 1995, pp.92–93.
[68] *Playing the congo / thumbpiano / akogo*:
https://www.youtube.com/watch?v=u_7e2sbetkU. Accessed 7 Feb. 2016.
[69] Loy 2006, p.72.

One of the earliest theories regarding microtonal tuning systems in the twentieth century was *Sonido 13* by Julian Carrillo (1875-1965). The French theorist M. Edmond Costere describes the tuning system of Carrillo's harp, which was made to produce 96 sounds in an octave, as a tuning system beyond the 53 Pythagorean comma.[70] Later Carrillo extended his theory in order to have unlimited intervals in an octave. This theory allowed Carrillo to find unlimited microtonal systems outside the 12-TET system range. He called his *Sonido 13* theory a revolution in musical sounds, intervals and harmonies.

The composer Alois Haba (1893–1973) wrote important theories about microtonal music.[71] In his book *New Theory of Harmony, of the Diatonic, the Chromic, the Quarter-tone, the Third-tone, the Sixth-tone, and the Twelfth-tone System*, he tried to find a relationship between the old Greek music and the new Western microtonal music. He composed for string instruments, which can precisely match his microtonal tuning system.[72] In order to match his systems to other instrumentations, he often modified existing instruments for his works, such as quartertone pianos.

In the twentieth century, many composers used microtonality in order to achieve new levels of expression. Among them were composers including Joseph Yasser (1893–1981) who wrote *A Theory of Evolving Tonality*, 1932;[73] Ivan Wyschnegradsky (1893–1979) who wrote *24 Preludes for quartertone pianos*; Harry Partch (1901–1974) who wrote *Delusion of the Fury* and other compositions using the Numerary Nexus way of tuning; Iannis Xenakis (1922–2001) who wrote *Metastasis*; and Gyorgy Ligeti (1923–2006) who wrote *Atmosphères*.

The music of Klaus Huber (b.1924) is of special significance for the theory. He is one of the composers who worked in merging Arabic microtonal music with Western music. He studied the classical Arabic music writings in the 1990s, and has composed pieces based on the *maqam*.[74]

In the 1970s, Heinz Bohlen (1910–2002) and John R. Pierce (1910–2002) used a scale based on the thirteenth root of three. This scale is constructed by using

---

[70] Carrillo, Julian. *Julian Carillo y el Sonido 13, Revolucion del Sonido 13*.
http://www.sonido13.com/sonido13.html, 11.07.2009. Accessed 7 Feb. 2016.
[71] Haba, Alois. *New Theory of Harmony, of the Diatonic, the Chromic, the Quarter-tone, the Third-tone, the Sixth-tone, and the Twelfth-tone System*. Universal Education A. G., Wien 1978, p.6–8.
[72] In his *Suite* for string orchestra (1917), he used quartertones for the first time.
[73] Nolan, Catherine. *Music theory and mathematics*. In *The Cambridge History of Music. The Cambridge History of Western Music Theory*. Thomas Christensen, ed. Cambridge UP, Cambridge 2008, p.297.
[74] Some examples from Klaus Huber's work where he merged Arabic microtonal music with Western music can be found in the following pieces: *Die Erde bewegt sich auf den Hörnern eines Ochsen*, and *Die Seele muss vom Reittier steigen*. Keller, Kjell. *Klaus Huber und die arabische Musik, Begegnungen, Entgrenzungen, Berührungen*. Dissonanz, no. 88, December, Basel 2004, pp.14–20.
(http://www.dissonance.ch/upload/pdf/088_14_hb_kjk_huber.pdf). Accessed 7 Feb. 2016.

a high harmonic value of 3:5:7,[75] and is another example of the Bohlen-Pierce scale. High harmonic values can be adapted in the light of this theory.

In the 1970s a new musical school called *Les Spectraux* was established in France. The main goal of the school was that its composers would use the acoustic properties of sound itself, or sound spectra, as the basis of their compositional material.[76] The composers of that school, Gérard Grisey (1946–1998), Hugues Dufourt (b.1943), Tristan Murail (b.1947), Michael Levinas (b.1949), Roger Tessier (b.1939), and Claude Viver (1948–1983), used different kinds of tuning systems, such as the 12-TET and the 24-TET. Their studies of the music of the spectralists play an important role for the development of my theory because these studies offer the possibility of connecting Western music with Arabic music. As a composer from the Arabic world with a universal musical vision, I direct my work towards:
- Searching for new harmonic techniques that can fit Arabic music;
- Applying the *maqam* idea as a horizontal gesture to verticality on a spectral background;
- Searching for a new microtonal theory that can serve these aims.

3.2 Spectral- and overtone-music

3.2.1 Spectral music

From a general point of view, music is by nature spectral. Only in the second part of the twentieth century did composers start focusing on music's spectral properties as a source for compositional techniques; however, the inspiring element for spectral music had been present in the traditional music of different cultures as overtone music. This overtone music can be performed without the use of special techniques by instruments such as the didgeridoo, the bucium, the tilinca, the Carpathian horn, the alphorn, the bamboo overtone flute, the jaw harp, or as overtone singing such as Tuvan throat singing in Mongolia, *umnqokolo*, *umngqokolo* and *ngomqangi* throat singing style in South Africa, Inuit throat singing *katajjaq* from Canada, *rekuhkara* in Russia, Ainu from Japan, and throat singing in *tenore* songs in Sardinian.

In Western music, Olivier Messiaen (1908–1992) inspired his students by giving them the idea that the future of music could lie in the sound itself.[77] He created special types of chords he called *accord de résonance*, which are combinations of pitches belonging to a fundamental located in inaudible regions.

Following Messian, a group of composers calling themselves *Les Spectraux* was formed in Paris. Many composers, before and after, worked in the field of

---

[75] Walker 2001.
[76] Anderson 2001, p.166.
[77] Fineberg, Joshua. *Classical Music, Why Bother?* Routledge, London 2006, p.134.

spectral music, among them Ferruccio Busoni (1866–1924),[78] Claude Debussy (1862–1918),[79] Edgard Varèse (1883–1965), Béla Bartók (1881–1945), György Ligeti (1923–2006),[80] Iannis Xenakis (1922–2001). These composers are now referred to as proto-spectral composers.[81]

Karlheinz Stockhausen (1928–2007) composed *Stimmung* in 1968. This 70-minute piece is based on one chord, the B ninth chord. The singers perform overtones up to the twenty-fourth of this harmonic series (B). *Stimmung* was one of the first major works to influence the French spectralists.[82] The importance of this piece is the way he wrote pitches in spectral harmonics, as well as the relationship between these harmonics and time.

Per Nørgård's *Voyage into the Golden Screen* for chamber orchestra (1968) is another example of what can be called a protospectral work.[83]

The term spectral music was first used by Dufourt in an article in 1979.[84] As a representative of *Les Spectraux,* Tristan Murail gave a clear definition of spectral music in his lecture in Darmstadt in 1980.[85] He defined spectral music as a way of thinking, rather than as a technique, yet the main method for composing according to the principles of spectral music is the employment of harmonic overtones.[86] All spectral music is based on the analysis of a complex sound wave by breaking it down into a waveform. The sound waves are transferred by the Fourier Transform FFT[87] into simple sine waves that can be seen in a spectrogram.[88] All degrees of frequencies are represented in different frequency categories. These frequencies are converted into musical pitches by comparing them to the equal temperament tuning-systems, 12-TET,[89] 17-TET, 24-TET.

Georg Hajdu[90] developed the software *Macaque* in order to transform acoustic sounds into scores by projecting features of the spectrum into pitches. The

---

[78] cf. Busoni, Ferruccio. *Entwurf einer neuen Ästhetik der Tonkunst.* Insel, Frankfurt am Main 1974, p.44.
[79] Mabury, Brett. *An investigation into the spectral music idiom and its association with visual imagery particularly that of film and video.* http://ro.ecu.edu.au/cgi/viewcontent.cgi?article=1129&context=theses, 30 Jun. 2006. Accessed 7 Feb. 2016.
[80] See Ligeti, György Sándo. *Lontano.* Schott, Mainz 1967, bars 1–6.
[81] Fineberg 2006, p.123.
[82] Anderson 2001, vol.24, p.166.
[83] Fineberg 2006, p.123.
[84] Cornicello, Anthony. *Timbral Organization in Tristan Murail's "Désintégrations" and "Rituals."* PhD thesis. Brandeis University, Massachusetts 2000, p.2.
[85] Pasler, Jann. *Writing Through Music.* Oxford UP, Oxford 2008, p.82.
[86] Fineberg 2006, p.116.
[87] FFT: Fast Fourier Transform, a clever implementation of the DFT (Discrete Fourier Transform) Sethares 2005, p.xvii.
[88] A photographic or other visual or electronic time varying representation of a spectrum.
[89] TET: equal temperament tuning system.
[90] Hajdu, Georg. Official website: http://georghajdu.de/6-2/macaque/ Accessed 7 Feb. 2016.

process opens an audio analysis data in audio analyzer software like *SPEAR*[91] or *AudioSculp*. The software represents the data in many individual sinusoidal tracks. These data are saved as SDIF[92] files and then opened in the MaxScore object,[93] which transforms the information into scores.[94]

Gérard Grisey's *Partiels* (1975) is an early example of spectral music. He built a spectrum harmonic series pitches using the E on the trombone. Tristan Murail's *Gondwana*, for full orchestral, was published in 1980. Murail has used many different techniques of spectral composition and also included the non-spectral white noise by using extended techniques, such as scratching and *col legno* effects. He also used a special technique to create bell and brass sounds.[95]

Between 1980 and 2000 many ensembles were founded to explore spectral music. One of the first and the most prominent was the French Ensemble l'Itinéraire, which was mainly found by Gérard Grisey, Tristan Murail, Michaël Levinas, Hugues Dufourt.[96]

Many Romanian composers have worked extensively with spectral techniques. Important names include Horațiu Rădulescu (1942–2008), Iancu Dumitrescu (b.1944), Stefan Niculescu (1927–2008), Călin Ioachimescu (b.1949), and Aurel Stroe (1932–2008). The Hyperion Ensemble (1976) was founded and conducted by Iancu Dumitrescu to perform spectral music. Dumitrescu, like most other spectralists, also composed computer music. One of his recent works is *Étude Granulaire*, which is spectral-computer assisted music. The relationship between spectralist and computer music is an important source for their inspiration.

In Germany Erhard Grosskopf (b.1934), has carried out a great deal of research about consonance in.[97] His works include *Quintett über den Herbstanfang* for orchestra (1981/82) and *Slow motion* (1981).

---

[91] Klingbeil, Michael. *SPEAR* software program. http://www.klingbeil.com/spear/ Accessed 7 Feb. 2016.

[92] Schwarz, Diemo & Matthew Wright. SDIF (The Sound Description Interchange Format): *Extensions and Applications of the SDIF Sound Description Interchange Format*. Proceedings of the International Computer Music Conference, Ircam 2000.
http://recherche.ircam.fr/anasyn/schwarz/publications/icmc2000/sdif-extensions.pdf, 2000. Accessed 7 Feb. 2016.

[93] MaxScore is a Max/Msp object which accepts messages that can create a score, add notes to it, perform it, save it, load it, and export the score to popular formats for professional publishable results.
Max/Msp is an environmental program written in Java programming language, used mostly by musicians and multimedia artists.

[94] Fineberg 2006, p.119.

[95] Gérard Grisey also used electronic sonogram device to analyze E2 pitch in his work *partiels*, Fineberg 2006, p.116.

[96] Ensemble l'Itinéraire was founded in 1973 by Adrian Pereyra, Gérard Grisey, Michâel Levinas, Hughes Doufourt and Philippe Hurel.

[97] Some composers work on the time track: they divide their time by events on their schedule that are important to them. To me, such music always seems to exist in one dimension, especially because the events, threaded on to a time string, usually follow an old dramaturgy. I believe that

Two other important figures are the English composers Jonathan Harvey (b. 1939) and Trevor Wishart (b.1946). Jonathan Harvey joined the Ensemble l'Itinéraire, and provided the concrete sounds of the deep church bell tones and the boy soprano for the computer generated pieces *Mortuos Plango* and *Vivos Voco* (1980). In *Vox 5* (1986), Trevor Wishart combined the sounds of two unexpected partners: a horse's whinny and a baby's cry.[98]
Electronic music, computer music, avant-garde, and electro-acoustic music have a strong parallel to the Western classical instrumental music in spectral composition, as McAdams and Matzkin explain:

> "Finally, we should not leave out the realm of electroacoustic music in which spectral and temporal sound structures can be imagined from scratch and become the basis for compositional development or in which recorded sounds can become musical materials in their own right as the composer delves into and transforms the inner structure of the sound itself."[99]

3.2.2 Overtone music in western avant-garde

In western avant-garde music there are many ways to use overtones. Composers like Liza Lim, Gerd Kühr and Philemon Mukarno used acoustic instruments while electronic music was used by Wolfgang Martin Stroh in his work *MIDI-Planetarium*. Computer music was used by James Tenney in *Ergodos I*. Human voices producing overtones based on fundamental tones were used by David Hykes in his ensemble The Harmonic Choir since 1975.
One of the most famous types of overtone music to influence western overtone music is Tuvan throat singing. This form of singing established a new method of singing in the west called *Xoomei* (or *khoomi*). Robert Zollitsch, Wolfgang Saus, Marco Tonini, Jens Mügge and other western musicians have been inspired by the *Xoomei* technique of singing and worked in the field of western overtone music.

3.3 Fusions of Western and Arabic music

In the twentieth century, Western music began to attract musicians from the Arabic world through its harmonies, forms, instruments, techniques. The *maqam* in Arabic music is an example of this; the oriental touch proved very attractive to Western composers. There are many examples of the influence of Eastern music upon Western composers. At the turn of the twentieth century,

---

sounds, when they appear, have their own meaning. They contain a kind of time energy that in connection with sound constellations of multi-layered processes transform musical time into a spatial dimension.
[98] McAdams, Stephen & Daniel Matzkin. *The Roots of Musical Variation in Perceptual Similarity and Invariance*. In *The Cognitive Neuroscience of Music*: Isabelle Peretz & Robert J. Zatorre, eds., Oxford UP, 2003, p.81.
[99] McAdams & Matzkin 2003, p.2.

works such as *Aida* (1871) by Giuseppe Verdi or *Scheherazade* (1910) by Nicolai Rimsky- Korsakov reflected a fascination with non-European musical worlds, but on a rather superficial level in regard to grammatical structure by imitating the atmosphere of Arabic music, without going deep in its tuning system and musical forms. Many years later, Klaus Huber (b. 1924) succeeded in developing scales belonging to the Arabic music system and applied them to Western compositional techniques.

After the first Arabic Music Congress in Cairo in 1932, Arabic musicians adapted the western 24-TET tuning system to document their music. Since the 1960s many classical Arabic singers including Abdel Halim Hafez and Umm Kulthum, and composers Mohammad Abdel Wahab and Mohammed Al-Mougy used instruments such as keyboards, accordion, electronic musical instruments and other western instruments, although the music was for the Arabic *maqamat*. Recently attention has been paid to fusing Arabic and Western music and instruments; for instance, the Arabic jazz of Ziad Rahbani, Rabih Abou-Khalil, Leena Shamamian, and the popular music of Cheb Khaled and Cheb Mami.

The traditional music of ethnic communities was not far from this fusion; it was renewed using the 24-TET keyboard as found in the music of Omar Souleyman, Ali Al Deek, Wafiq Habib. Until now, this fusion has been without recourse to a theoretical background.

4 Performing practice of microtonal music

4.1 From 24-TET to 240-TET

Musicians use a number of accidentals to aid musical notation. One of the aims is to write the intervals between tones in a way that is easy to read and perform.[100] The 1932 Arabic Music Congress[101] proposed use of the following accidentals in the notation of Arabic music in order to describe the displacements of tones of less than a semitone:

♭ lowers a tone by a quarter tone

♯ raises a tone by a quarter tone

In addition to the semitones accidentals:

♭ lowers a tone by a half tone

♯ raises a tone by a half tone

These accidentals present the Arabic music as a 24-TET, which is a hypothetical result of the congress. This is because musicians and theorists have always found small differences in the intervals in the music of Arabic countries, and even of within cities of the same country.[102] Musicians and theorists have come to recognise that music in Turkey uses the following accidentals in notation:

♯ raises a tone by a one ninth

♯ raises a tone by a four-ninths

♯ raises a tone by a five-ninths

♯ raises a tone by a eight-ninths

𝕩 double sharp a nine-ninths, or a tone higher

♭ lowers a tone by one-ninth

♭ lowers a tone by four-ninths

♭ lowers a tone by five-ninths

---

[100] See Karkoschka, Erhard. *Notation in New Music*. Universal Education, London 1972, pp.2–3, 27–28.
[101] مؤتمر الموسيقى العربية الذي عقد في القاهرة سنة ١٩٣٢/Mutamar Almusiqa Alarabieh 1932. *The Arabic Music Congress in Cairo in 1932,* Al-amieria, Cairo 1932, p. m99.
[102] El-Mahdi, Salah. *la Musique Arabe*, Alphonse Leduc, Paris 1972, pp.36–38.

𝄭 lowers a tone by eight-ninths

𝄫 double flat a tone lower, or nine-ninths

Salah El-Mahdi came to a different evaluation for the intervals in the different *maqamat*. He compared the different intervals in *maqam* music in different cultures, for example the intervals of the Arabic and Persians *maqam* follow the quarter-tone theory and the Turkish one follow the one-ninth tone. In 1968 he attended a conference with three other researches from Turkey, Iran, and Lebanon and they agreed that some intervals can be lower or higher by twenty, thirty, or forty percent.[103]

Umar Abd-Al-Rahman Al-Humssi [104] in his book *The Origin of the Oriental Rhythms and an Analysis Study in the Arabic Maqamat*, divides the octave according to the *maqam* notation names. [105] For example, the names of the notes between *C* and *D* are:

Rast | Semi-Nim Zircula | Nim Zircula | Minor-Zircula | Major-Zircula | Semi-Tic Zircula | Tic Zircula | Minor-Dokah | Dokah

Figure 10: Names of the intervals within a major second (from *C* to *D*) in Arabic Music.

These eight intervals within a major second lead to 46 intervals within an octave. [106] Apart from Al-Humssi, the traditional tuning system in Arabic music theory subdivides the scale into 53 intervals referred to as the *Arabic comma*, which was developed in the eighth century from the Pythagorean tuning system.[107]

As mentioned above, following the Arabic Music Congress in Cairo in 1932, it was suggested that Arabic music be notated in the 24-TET, even though the Arabic *maqam* system has about 53 divisions,[108] each of which is distinguished by its own name.

---

[103] El-Mahdi 1972, p.18.

[104] عمر عبد الرحمن الحمصي Al-Humssi, Umar Abd-Al-Rahman.

أصول الإيقاعات الشرقية ودراسة تحليلية في المقامات العربية / *Usool Aliqaat Alsharqieh ua Diraseh Tahlilieh fi al-Maqamat Alarabieh*/ *The Origin of the Oriental Rhythms and an Analysis Study in the Arabic Maqamat*. Al-Assad Library-Press, Damascus 1992, p.177.

[105] He called it the *Arabic Scale*; it is more of a microtonal chromatic scale.

[106] 8*6=46, eight intervals in a major second, in the octave there are six major seconds.

[107] Touma 2003, p.22.

[108] I am using the term (about) because each maqam has its own intervals, so the $E^\natural$ in *jins Rast* is not the same as the $E^\natural$ in *jins Sika* nor the $E^\natural$ in *jins Bayat*. Further, each culture has its measurement for the intervals in the *ajnas* of the *maqam*.

Both systems are used in my theory. The first one, 24-TET, can be seen as an easy way for musicians to read and to perform. The second one, 72-TET, is more precise and better suited for use with overtone music.

Theoretically a composer can go down to about 400-TET, because the human ear barely notices a pitch difference of 2 or 3 cents.[109]

The 72-TET has 72 intervals, each of which has ~16.7 cents. I use both 24-TET and 72-TET tuning systems, which share the accidentals (♮,♯,♯, ♭,♭):

Accidentals used in my composition.
Divisions between *C* and *D* in the 24-TET.

Figure 11: Accidentals used in my composition.
Divisions between *C* and *D* in the 72-TET.

The 72-TET is very well adapted to my Spectral Microtonal Music and it is easy for musicians to read on the score.

The 1200-TET is used in the theory to clarify the precise intervals between the overtones, as well as for electronic music devices and computer music. These divisions are very small which makes it beyond what the ear can distinguish.

---

[109] Sethares 2005, p.44.
The just noticeable difference (JND) is the smallest microtonal interval that can be distinguished by the human ear. An octave with 1200cents, which can be divided into 1200/3=400 divisions or 1200/2=600 divisions, depends on the sound pressure level (Decibel). Parker, Barry R. *Good Vibrations*. Johns Hopkins UP, Baltimore 2009, p.36–38.

4.2 Properties of the overtone series

The overtone series of certain tone,[110] for example C1, can be represented by pitches. These pitches have the same frequency of the waves or overtones and can be calculated as follows:

---

[110] Sine or cosine waves.

Overtone Frequency in Hz	Deviation from 12-TET in Cent	Frequency in Hz	Intervals in Cents				
1-	C1	32.703	2400	69-	C# +30	2256.512	9730
2-	C2	65.406	3600	70-	C# +55	2289.215	9755
3-	G2 +2	98.109	4302	71-	C# +80	2321.918	9780
4-	C3	130.812	4800	72-	D7 +4	2354.621	9804
5-	E3 -14	163.515	5186	73-	D +28	2387.324	9828
6-	G3 +2	196.218	5502	74-	D +51	2420.027	9851
7-	B3 -31	228.922	5769	75-	D +75	2452.731	9875
8-	C4	261.625	6000	76-	Es7 -2	2485.433	9898
9-	D4 +4	294.328	6204	77-	Es +20	2518.137	9920
10-	E4 -14	327.031	6386	78-	Es +43	2550.84	9943
11-	F4 +51	359.734	6551	79-	Es +65	2583.543	9965
12-	G4 +2	392.437	6702	80-	Es +86	2616.246	9986
13-	A4 -41	425.14	6841	81-	E7 +8	2648.949	10008
14-	B4 -31	457.843	6969	82-	E +29	2681.652	10029
15-	A#4 +88	490.546	7088	83-	E +50	52714.355	10050
16-	C5	523.249	7200	84-	E +71	2747.058	10071
17-	C#5 +5	555.952	7305	85-	F7 -9	2779.761	10091
18-	D5 +4	588.655	7404	86-	F7 +12	2812.464	10112
19-	D#5 -2	621.358	7498	87-	F +32	2845.167	10132
20-	E5 -14	654.061	7586	88-	F +51	2877.87	10151
21-	E5 +71	6 86.765	7671	89-	F +71	2910.573	10171
22-	F5 +51	719.468	7751	90-	F +90	2943.276	10190
23-	F#5 +28	752.171	7828	91-	F#7 +9	2975.98	10209
24-	G5 +2	784.874	7902	92-	F# +28	3008.683	10228
25-	A5 -27	817.577	7973	93-	F# +47	3041.386	10247
26-	A5 -59	850.28	8041	94-	F# +66	3074.089	10266
27-	A5 +6	882.983	8106	95-	F# +84	3106.792	10284
28-	B5 -31	915.686	8169	96-	G7 +02	3139.495	10302
29-	H5 -70	948.389	8230	97-	G +20	3172.198	10320
30-	H5 -12	981.092	8288	98-	G +38	3204.901	10338
31-	H5 +45	1013.795	8345	99-	G +55	3237.604	10355
32-	C6	1046.498	8400	100-	G +73	3270.307	10373
33-	C6 +53	1079.201	8453	101-	G +90	3303.01	10390
34-	C#6 +5	1111.904	8505	102-	As7 +7	3335.713	10407
35-	C# +55	1144.608	8555	103-	As7 +24	3368.416	10424
36-	D6 +4	1177.31	8604	104-	As7 +41	3401.119	10441
37-	D6 +51	1210.014	8651	105-	As7 +57	3433.823	10457
38-	Es6 -2	1242.717	8698	106-	As7 +74	3466.526	10474
39-	E6 -57	1275.42	8743	107-	A7 -10	3499.229	10490
40-	E6 -14	1308.123	8786	108-	A7 +6	3531.932	10506
41-	E6 +30	1340.826	8830	109-	A +22	3564.635	10522
42-	E6 +71	1373.529	8871	110-	A +38	3597.338	10538
43-	F6 +12	1406.232	8912	111-	A +53	3630.041	10553
44-	F +51	1438.935	8951	112-	A +69	3662.744	10569
45-	F +90	1471.638	8990	113-	A +84	3695.447	10584
46-	F#6 +28	1504.341	9028	114-	B7	3728.150	10600
47-	F#6 +66	1537.044	9066	115-	B7 +15	3760.853	10615
48-	G6 +2	1569.747	9102	116-	B7 +30	3793.556	10630
49-	As6 -62	1602.451	9138	117-	B7 +44	3826.26	10644
50-	As6 -27	1635.154	9173	118-	B7 +59	3858.962	10659
51-	As6 +7	1667.857	9207	119-	B7 +74	3891.666	10674
52-	A6 -59	1700.56	9241	120-	H7 -12	3924.369	10688
53-	A6 -26	1733.263	9274	121-	H7 +03	3957.072	10703
54-	A6 +6	1765.966	9306	122-	H +17	3989.775	10717
55-	B6 -62	1798.669	9338	123-	H +31	4022.478	10731
56-	B6 -31	1831.372	9369	124-	H +45	4055.181	10745
57-	B6	1864.075	9400	125-	H +59	4087.884	10759
58-	H6 -70	1896.778	9430	126-	H +73	4120.587	10773
59-	H6 -41	1929.481	9459	127-	H +86	4153.3	10786
60-	H6 -12	1962.184	9488	128-	C8	4186	10800
61-	H6 +17	1994.887	9517	129-	C +14	4185.993	10814
62-	H6 +45	2027.59	9545	130-	C +27	4218.696	10827
63-	H6 +73	2060.3	9573	131-	C +40	4251.399	10840
64-	C7	2093	9600	132-	C +53	4284.103	10853
65-	C +27	2125.7	9627	133-	C +66	4316.806	10866
66-	C +53	2158.403	9653	134-	C +79	4349.508	10879
67-	C +79	2191.106	9679	135-	C +92	4382.211	10892
68-	C#7 +5	2223.809	9705	136-	C#8 +15	4414.915	10905
				137-	C# +18	4447.618	10918
				138-	C# +30	4480.321	10930
				139-	C# +43	4513.024	10943
				140-	C# +55	4545.727	10955
				141-	C# +68	4578.43	10968

142-	C# +80	4611.133	10980
143-	C# +92	4643.836	10992
144-	D 8+4	4676.539	11004
145-	D +16	4709.242	11016
146-	D +28	4741.945	11028
147-	D +40	4774.648	11040
148-	D +51	4807.352	11051
149-	D +63	4840.055	11063
150-	D +75	4872.758	11075
151-	Es8 -14	4905.461	11086
152-	Es -2	4938.164	11098
153-	Es8 +9	4970.867	11109
154-	Es +20	5003.57	11120
155-	Es +31	5036.273	11131
156-	Es +43	5068.976	11143
157-	Es +54	5101.679	11154
158-	Es +65	5134.382	11165
159-	Es +76	5167.085	11176
160-	E8 -14	5199.789	11186
161-	E8 -3	5232.491	11197
162-	E8 +8	5265.194	11208
163-	E +19	5297.898	11219
164-	E +29	5330.601	11229
165-	E +40	5363.304	11240
166-	E +50	5396.007	11250
167-	E +60	5428.71	11260
168-	E +71	5461.413	11271
169-	E +81	5494.116	11281
170-	F8 -9	5526.819	11291
171-	F8 +1	5559.522	11301
172-	F +12	5592.225	11312
173-	F +22	5624.928	11322
174-	F +32	5657.631	11332
175-	F +42	5690.335	11342
176-	F +51	5723.038	11351
177-	F +61	5755.741	11361
178-	F +71	5788.444	11371
179-	F +81	5821.147	11381
180-	F +90	5853.85	11390
181-	F#8	5886.553	11400
182-	F# +9	5919.256	11409
183-	F# +19	5951.959	11419
184-	F# +28	5984.662	11428
185-	F# +38	6017.365	11438
186-	F# +47	6050.068	11447
187-	F# +56	6082.772	11456
188-	F# +66	6115.475	11466
189-	F# +75	6148.177	11475
190-	F# +84	6180.88	11484
191-	F# +93	6213.584	11493
192-	G8 +2	6246.287	11502

Table 6: First 192 overtones of a tone C1 (32.703 Hz) spectrum.

In this table, the numbers of overtones are in column 1. Their frequencies are in column 3, the consecutive intervals in cents are in column 4, and the deviation of the overtone pitches from the 12-TET are in column 2. In column 2 the deviation is written from the nearest tone to the 12-TET. Using the traditional western notation of music, the overtone series can be approximately written as follows:[111]

---

[111] The accidentals here are compared to the 72-TET which can be found in Figure **11**.

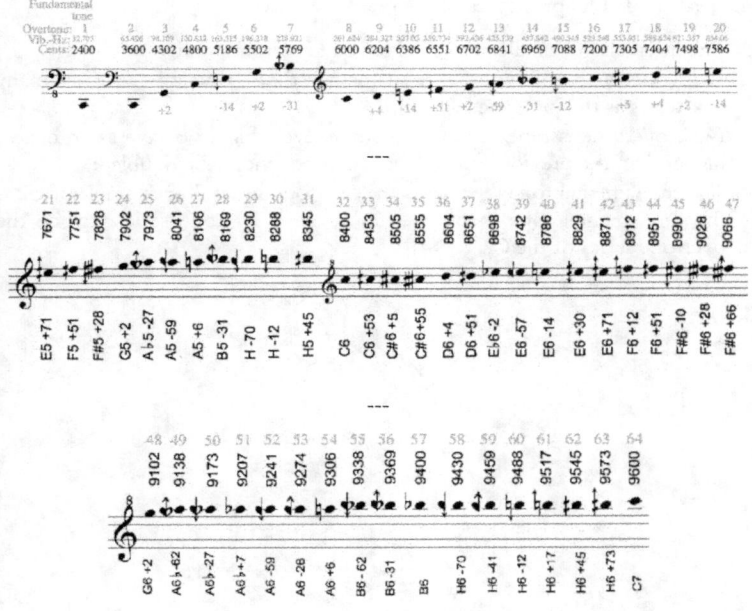

Figure 12: First 64 overtones converted to musical pitches of a fundamental tone C1 (32.703 Hz) spectrum.

The previous notation for the overtone series,[112] illustrated in Figure 12, is a representative term for the first 64 overtones of the harmonic series of a sound which starts from the fundamental and extend to the sixty-fourth overtone. These overtones are in natural ratio numbers excluding the zero.

The overtone series is an expression of the nature of the tone or timbre and appears as the structure of any harmonic sound, as with natural tones when an aerophone is overblown; or like partial tones when a string is divided into equal parts, or as a harmonic on a stringed instrument, or as a mathematical series, which is used to characterize, explain or legitimatize aesthetic theories on harmony, or the impact of music according to the philosophy that what is good or beautiful is simple and simple is what can be measured by small natural numbers.

---

[112] Olson, Harry F. *Music, Physics and Engineering*. Dover Publications, New York 1967, p.38.

The basic structural properties of the overtone series are:

- The intervals get smaller and smaller in a logarithmic way;
- Every octave up from the fundamental tone contains twice as many overtones as the lower octave;
- Each overtone is repeated in each successively higher octave as an octave higher than the previous one. Hence the frequency is be doubled;
- The fundamental tone represents the overtone series. For example, if C2 is the fundamental tone then the name of the overtone series will be the overtone series of the C2.

5 A theory of spectral music

When a composer aims to obtain special sounds, he searches in different ways to make changes in the sound whether in its properties including amplitude, period, frequency, and wavelength or in amplitudes of harmonics of the sound itself. Playing or singing a sound with a certain instrument or the human voice implies a special timbre of a tone. The changes of the timbre can be detected by a spectrogram. This spectrum can be changed in different ways; for example, it can be changed by altering dynamics piano (p) or forte (f). Also it can be affected by a change in the performing atmosphere conditions (cold or warm climate, humid or dry), or by changing our position towards the sound, etc.

Moreover, it is possible to obtain this effect in the sound by changing the amplitude of certain overtones. This involves keeping the same frequency of the overtones and changing the amplitude of highlighted overtones. This can result in a new timbre.

The previous procedures may also be applied to composed sounds. This means the previous procedure of a single sound can be simulated to get multi-sounds where the final artificial sound is the target.[113] An example of that is when a composer writes down tones for instruments playing at once, and the final sound is affected by:

- Changing the timbre of the instruments
- Changing the amplitudes of the sound of the instruments
- Changing the position of the musicians or the performing atmosphere. The humidity and the temperature of the room in addition to the musician position to the audience affect the timbre.

In general, the term Spectral Music describes all kinds of music that consist of microtones or micro-intervals referring to the overtone series in a structural way. Examples of spectral music using overtone include throat singing such as western overtone singing,[114] or spectral computer music with exact calculated pitches of the overtone series such as Stroh's *Midi-Planetarium* in which he uses exclusively the exact overtones.[115] Spectral microtonal music has more or less similar properties to music with electronically generated overtones. This theory is basically concentrated on the first 16 overtones for the microtonal overtone scale and on the first 32 overtones for the chromatic microtonal overtone scale.

This first stage of the theory forms the background, as detailed in the first four chapters of this book, and the main idea of the following part is spectral

---

[113] Bartolozzi, Bruno. *New Sounds for Woodwind*. Oxford University Press, Oxford 1967. p.12–14.
[114] Burt 2001, p.20, 142, 199.
[115] Stroh, Wolfgang M. Official website. http://www.musik-for.uni-oldenburg.de/planet/index1.html Accessed 7 Feb. 2016.

microtonal cross-cultural music. The second stage of my research cross-cultural study will handle Arabic music in relation to the contemporary microtonal and spectral music.

In my compositions, *maqamat* are used in a contemporary, atonal, spectral way, *maqam* contrapuntal movement in spectral form, or *maqam* harmony based on an overtone theory. This theory demonstrates possible ways of writing harmonies and melodies that can fit into the *maqamat*.

5.1 Overtone music in practice

5.1.1 The relationship of the overtones resultant from tones when they are played simultaneously or successively

The amplitude of the overtones of a tone is important in defining its timbre.[116] The timbre of the sound can be distinguished in different ways or different volumes, and the tone will have a different timbre so that the amplitude of the overtones will be different.

Taking this into consideration, the first 16 overtones will be used as a basis to give the sound its timbre. By observing the overtones of many musical instruments, as is demonstrated in the Figures 14 and 15, we notice the importance of the first 16 overtones in giving the sound its timbre. The pitch takes its name from the fundamental tone, assuming that it has high amplitude. The amplitudes of the other fifteen overtones will decrease in order from the fundamental as is shown in the hypothetical spectrum graph (Figure 13):

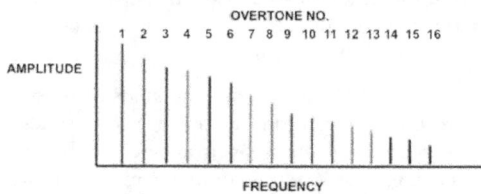

Figure 13: Hypothetical spectrum paragraph of 16 overtones.

The reasons for choosing these 16 overtones are related to extensive experiments and hypotheses of researchers who have worked in the field of acoustics and tuning-systems.

These reasons can be summarized by the following arguments:

Observation 1:

Comparing the higher octaves and the lower octaves of the overtones of a spectrum of selected musical instruments, we can see that the significance of

---

[116] Parker 2009, p.67.

the overtone dB[117] depends strongly on its position. As Loy observes, "[f]or many vibrating systems (but not all), the higher the mode, the less energy it has."[118]

The following are examples for tone spectrums for violin, bassoon, and nai:

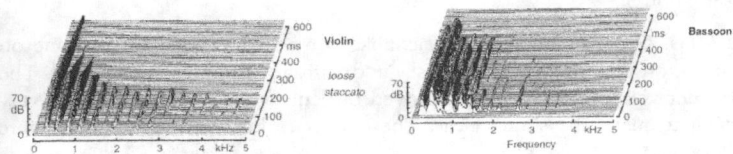

Figure 14: Observed measurements of tone spectrum developments in time for three C4 staccato tones[119].

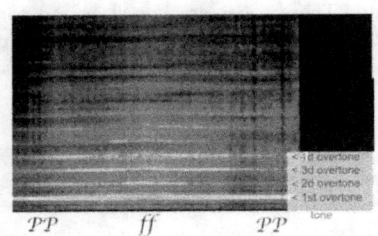

Figure 15: Sonogram showing the low D on a Nai[120] played crescendo and then diminuendo. The brightness indicates to the amplitude of the overtones. The fundamental tone is the first overtone.

The previous figures show that in general the first overtones have higher amplitudes than the upper ones.

Observation 2:

The amplitudes of the first sixteen overtones of a tone are essential to determine a sound's timbre.[121]

Take, for example, A4 (440Hz) played by a clarinet, and put this tone into a spectrogram like SPEAR to determine its spectrum. All overtones which have vibrations higher than the sixteenth overtone (7040 Hz)[122] are deleted, and we

---

[117] dB, Decibel: The relation of a certain sound pressure to a reference value.
[118] Loy 2006, p.30.
[119] Myer, Jürgen. *Acoustics and the Performance of Music*. Springer, Braunschweig 2009, p.25.
[120] Nai, also Ney or Nay, is a traditional musical Arabic instrument. This experiment was performed using Max/MSP program.
[121] Parker 2009, p.66.
[122] 440Hz*16 = 7040 Hz.

find that we are still able to recognize the clarinet sound and that the sound can be heard clearly.

Conversely, if we delete all overtones lower than the sixteenth overtone the first thing we notice is that the sound is no longer clear, and is very weak and, compared to the first, has lost its timbre.

Observation 3:

The cellist Graham Waterhouse was able to reach the sixteenth overtone on the cello, on the C string, quite easily and with a reasonably clear sound. The subsequent overtones, however, proved difficult to perform, and it was very difficult to make the sound clear. The overtones beyond the twentieth were unplayable.

Observation 4:

It is almost impossible to play more than four octaves with one fingering on woodwind instruments. These tones are not clear and some of them will be difficult to play. For example, the flute can use the same fingering for four tones that have the same pitch: C4, C5, C6, and C7, but only the first two are clear.

Observation 5:

The fundamental tone gives the pitch its name, although sometimes it can be missed in the spectral representation.[123] Therefore, I found that it would be logical to construct a scale that starts and ends with the same fundamental pitch.

Observation 6:

There is evidence in the Sygryt style of Tuvan throat singing that the singer can reach the thirteenth overtone (see Figure 106). [124]

Observation 7:

Many tuning system theories are based on constructing intervals within a scale with small natural numbers in the numerators and denominators of the tone ratios. This means that theorists construct their tuning system relying on intervals from the next-to-lower overtones in the harmonic series. Just intonation systems can be an example for many theories in tuning systems based on overtone series with small natural numbers in the numerators and denominators of the tone ratios. The tuning systems of the Chinese, the Indian, and the Arabic

---

[123] Tramo, Mark Jude, et al.. *Neurobiology of Harmony Perception*. In Peretz & Zatorre, Oxford 2003, p.136.
[124] *Huun Huur Tu at Philadelphia Folk Festival, August 2006*:
(http://www.youtube.com/watch?v=RxK4pQgVvfg, uploaded by tantsev, on 15.09.2006) Accessed 7 Feb. 2016.

cultures use the Pythagorean tuning system theory or similar 3-limit tuning-systems.

Observation 8:

The pitches of the overtones of the lower octaves of a spectrum are repeated in the higher levels; the thing that makes them dominant.
The fundamental is repeated each 2^n times: 1, 2, 4, 8, 16, then comes the third repeated each $3*2^n$ times: 3, 6, 12, 24 (n is a natural-number, $n \geq 0$).
If the first 16 tones are divided into octaves, four octaves result, and the fundamental pitch repeats itself four more times in the higher octaves. The third overtone pitch is repeated two more times. The fifth and the seventh pitches are repeated once more in the higher octave. The rest of the pitches are not repeated.
When the first 16 overtones are played as pitches, the fundamental pitch is repeated four times in the following overtones: 2, 4, 8, and 16; the third overtone pitch is repeated twice in the overtones 6 and 12; the fifth overtone pitch is repeated one time in the overtone 10; and the seventh overtone pitch will be repeated one time in the overtone 14. The remaining overtone pitches (9, 11, 13 and 15) are not repeated.
This is one of the reasons for the dominance of the fundamental pitch, as it is repeated more often than the other overtone pitches within the four octaves.
For example, the pitch of the fundamental tone of the C1 spectrum dominates the other overtone pitches because it is repeated in the second overtone as C2, in the fourth overtone as C3, in the eighth overtone as C4 and in the sixteenth overtone as C5.
The pitch of third overtone, G2, comes in the second class with two more repetitions in the sixth overtone as G3 and in the twelfth overtone as G4. The other overtone pitches have fewer repetitions or none.

All pitches that exist in the fourth octave of the harmonic series exist also in the lower octaves of the same series, the first, the second and the third octaves. These pitches have even numbers in the fourth octave while the new pitches in the fourth octave which do not exist in the lower octaves have odd numbers (Figure 16):

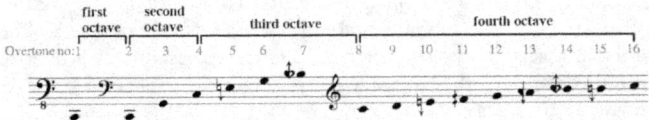

Figure 16: First four octaves of the overtone series.

In general, the outcome of this theory classifies the amplitude of hypothetical overtones in a harmonic series counting the position from the fundamental that has higher amplitude than the other overtones.

The string of the first 16 overtones can be simulated to a tree where the fundamental tone stands for the trunk of the tree while the branches are represented in the overtones in which the strong branches are the low ones (Figure 17):

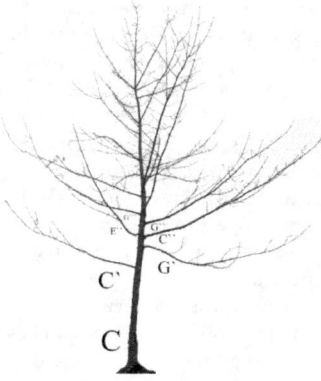

Figure 17: Illustration for a symbolic tree comparing it with the overtones of the sound, where the strength of the tree is mainly in the trunk and the branches are weaker. The trunk presents the fundamental tone and the branches are the overtones.

From the above reasons, this theory concentrates on the low overtones, presuming that they have more amplitude than the higher ones. This information will be also helpful for orchestration and for writing the dynamics of the pitches.

5.1.2 The microtonal overtone scale (M.O.S.)

If we gather the pitches that appear in the first 16 overtones (see Figure 16) in a scale that starts on the fundamental pitch and ends one octave higher, then we shall have a scale consisting of nine pitches representing all overtones in the first four octaves of the overtone series (Figure 18). This scale is called the microtonal overtone scale.

All the pitches of this scale exist in the fifth octave of the overtone series; the difference between them is the relationship of each of them with the fundamental. This relationship is based on two aspects:

1) The distance from the fundamental, and

2) The repetition of each pitch in the first four octaves of the harmonic series. Each pitch of this scale has a special categorization relating to the theory of the overtones loudness. [125]

Figure 18: Categorizing the pitches of the first four octaves of the overtone series due to their strength and the microtonal overtone scale.

This scale can be also considered a tuning system, if some tone is chosen from it to form a smaller scale. For example, in the Sygyt style of Tuvan throat singing) the scale used contains the following overtones: 7, 8, 9, 10, 12, and 13.[126]
The microtonal overtone scale is the basis of the theory, upon which melodies, harmonies and modulation are based.

5.1.3 The chromatic microtonal overtone scale (C.M.O.S.)

The range of the microtonal overtone scale is limited because it is based on eight pitches (8/8, 8/9, 8/10, 8/11, 8/12, 8/13, 8/14, 8/15, 8/16) that exist in the fourth octave of the harmonic series. For this reason, modulation is an essential method that I use to enrich the music with variable microtonal and overtonal elements.[127]
It is possible to enrich the M.O.S. and to give it wider range, greater variety of pitches, and more melodic choices by searching for extra tones that can be placed, respectively, between the tones of the M.O.S.
In the process of building a suitable C.M.O.S. it is necessary to preserve the correct values of the frequencies of the microtones of the overtone scale as much as possible. Thus, the chromatic pitches should be placed between the eight microtonal overtone scale pitches. This means that the C.M.O.S. should be composed of 16 pitches, as well as the sixth octave of the overtone series (Figure 12). The sixth octave contains the entire chromatic pitches of the C.M.O.S, which consists of the eight pitches of the M.O.S multiplied by 2 (even numbers: 16, 18, 20, 22, 24, 26, 28, 30, 32) in addition to eight pitches exist in the fourth octave (odd numbers: 17, 19, 21, 23, 25, 27, 29, 31):

---

[125] There are other theorists who led similar studies about the energy in the sound like Partch's kithara. Partch, Harry: *Genesis of a Music*. Da Capo Press, New York 1974; Schuler 2007–08, p.224.
[126] See Figure 106.
[127] See Figure 18.

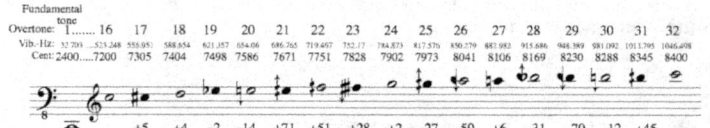

Figure 19: Chromatic microtonal overtone scale which is placed in the sixth octave of the C1 overtone series. The bright tones represent the microtonal overtones and the dark tones represent the new overtones. These new overtones in the microtonal overtone scale is placed an octave higher than the overtone scale in the fifth octave in the overtone series.

The chromatic overtones give the musical work more tone variety, but they have less effective sound amplitude in harmonics melody and in modulation[128] than the microtonal overtone scale. The extra microtones in C.M.O.S. are found on a weak range of the harmonic series from the seventeenth to the thirty-second overtone. The amplitude of the microtones of the microtonal overtone scale decreases from lowest to highest, so overtone 19 has less amplitude than overtone 17, and overtone 21 has less amplitude than overtone 19, and so on.

For the reason of sound amplitude, this theory concentrates on the use of the microtonal overtone scale and its modulation rather than on the chromatic microtonal overtone scale. Furthermore, the chromatic pitches of the microtonal overtone scale are used to replenish and to accomplish the aesthetic background of the microtonal overtone scale theory.

The main physical idea about both scales M.O.S. and C.M.O.S. is that all the overtones of the harmonic series that they belong to share the same two notes of the fundamental tone: [129]

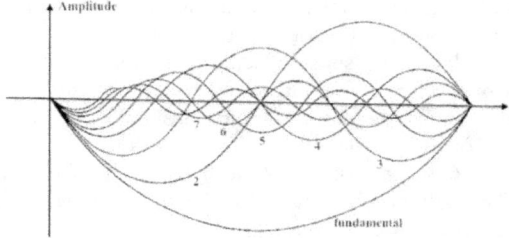

The overtones of a harmonic series

---

[128] See Chapter 5.1.1.
[129] Figure: Joly, Gordon. *The Six Senses*. http://sense-think-act.org/index.php?title=Senses, 13 Oct. 2004. Accessed 7 Feb. 2016. Modified figure by R.Ch.

5.1.4 The main overtone series,[130] derived fundamental tone and the branch overtone series

If a musician is asked to play a certain pitch then that pitch shall have tone. This tone has a harmonic series (the main harmonic series), and this harmonic has a fundamental tone (main fundamental tone) which has a similar frequency to pitch.

If another musician or a group of musicians is asked to play one or more of the overtones of the main harmonic series as tones, a new harmonic series known as the branch harmonic series results. Each instrument will play a derived fundamental tone which is an overtone in the main harmonic series.

For example, if a musician plays the tone C1 and a second musician plays the third overtone $G2_{+2cents}$, the third overtone and the tone $G2_{+2cents}$ have the same frequency. $G2_{+2cents}$ will be a fundamental tone for the new harmonic series. At the same time it will also be a derived fundamental tone for the harmonic series of C1 because it presents the third overtone of its harmonic series.

See the tables below:

---

[130] I also call it a mother tone harmonic series or original tone harmonic series.

Overtone No.	Deviation from 12-TET in Cent	The frequency of the main harmonic series	The f of the branch harm. ser. No.2	The f of the branch harm. ser. No.3	The f of the branch harm. ser. No.4	The f of the branch harm. ser. No.5	The f of the branch harm. ser. No.6	The f of the branch harm. ser. No.7	The f of the branch harm. ser. No.8	The f of the branch harm. ser. No.9	The f of the branch harm. ser. No.10	The f of the branch harm. ser. No.11	The f of the branch harm. ser. No.12	The f of the branch harm. ser. No.13	The f of the branch harm. ser. No.14	The f of the branch harm. ser. No.15	The f of the branch harm. ser. No.16
1.	C1	32.703															
2.	G2 +2	65.406															
3.		98.109															
4.		130.812															
5.	E3 -14	163.515	163.515														
6.	G3 +2	196.218	196.218	196.218													
7.	B3 -31	228.921															
8.	C4	261.624	261.624						261.624								
9.	D4 +4	294.328	294.328	294.327													
10.	E4 -14	327.03	327.03	327.03													
11.	F4 +51	359.733															
12.	G4 +2	392.436	392.436	392.436	392.436		392.436						392.436				
13.	A4 -59	425.139												425.139			
14.	B4 -31	457.842	457.842					457.842							457.842		
15.	H4-12	490.546		490.545		490.545										490.545	
16.		523.248	523.248		523.248												
17.	C#5 +5	555.951															
18.	D5 +44	588.654	588.654	588.654			588.654			588.654							
19.	D#5 -2	621.357															
20.	E5 -14	654.06	654.060								654.06						
21.	E5 +71	686.763		686.763				686.763									
22.	F5 +51	719.466	719.466									719.466					
23.	F#5 +28	752.169															
24.	G5 +2	784.872	784.872	784.872	784.872		784.872		784.872				784.872				
25.	A5 -27	817.575				817.575											
26.	A5 +59	850.28	850.278														
27.	A5 +6	882.981	882.981	882.981						882.981							
28.	B5 -31	915.684	915.684		915.6844			915.684							915.684		
29.	H5 -70	948.387															
30.	H5 -12	981.09	981.09	981.09		981.09	981.09				981.09					981.09	
31.	H5 +46	1013.793															
32.	C6	1046.496	1046.496	1046.496	1046.496				1046.496			1046.496					1046.496
33.		1079.2	1079.199	1079.199								1079.199					
34.	C#6 +5	1111.902	1111.902														
35.	C#6 +55	1144.605	1144.605			1144.605		1144.605									
36.	D6 +4	1177.308	1177.308	1177.308	1177.308		1177.308			1177.308			1177.308				
37.	D6 +51	1210.011															
38.	Es6 -2	1242.714	1242.714														
39.	E6 -14	1275.417		1275.417										1275.417			
40.	E6 +30	1308.12	1308.12		1308.12				1308.12								
41.	E6 +71	1340.823															
42.	F6 +12	1373.526	1373.526	1373.526			1373.526	1373.526							1373.526		
43.	F6 +51	1406.229															
44.	F +51	1438.932	1438.932		1438.932												
45.	F +90	1471.635	1471.635	1471.635		1471.635				1471.635						1471.635	
46.	F#6 +28	1504.338	1504.338														
47.	F#6 +66	1537.041															

Overtone No.	Deviation from 12-TET in Cent	The frequency of the main harmonic series	The *f* of the branch harm. ser. No.2	The *f* of the branch harm. ser. No.3	The *f* of the branch harm. ser. No.4	The *f* of the branch harm. ser. No.5	The *f* of the branch harm. ser. No.6	The *f* of the branch harm. ser. No.7	The *f* of the branch harm. ser. No.8	The *f* of the branch harm. ser. No.9	The *f* of the branch harm. ser. No.10	The *f* of the branch harm. ser. No.11	The *f* of the branch harm. ser. No.12	The *f* of the branch harm. ser. No.13	The *f* of the branch harm. ser. No.14	The *f* of the branch harm. ser. No.15	The *f* of the branch harm. ser. No.16
48-	G6 +2	1569.744	1569.744	1569.744	1569.744	-	1569.744	-	1569.744	-	-	-	1569.744	-	-	-	1569.744
49-	As6 -62	1602.447	-	-	-	-	-	1602.447	-	-	-	-	-	-	-	-	-
50-	As6 -27	1635.15	1635.15	-	-	1635.15	-	-	-	-	1635.15	-	-	-	-	-	-
51-	As6 +7	1667.853	-	1667.853	-	-	-	-	-	-	-	-	-	-	-	-	-
52-	A6 -59	1700.556	1700.556	-	1700.556	-	-	-	-	-	-	-	-	1700.556	-	-	-
53-	A6 -26	1733.259	-	-	-	-	-	-	-	-	-	-	-	-	-	-	-
54-	A6 +6	1765.962	1765.962	1765.962	-	-	1765.962	-	-	1765.962	-	-	-	-	-	-	-
55-	B6 -62	1798.665	-	-	-	1798.665	-	-	-	-	-	1798.665	-	-	-	-	-
56-	B6 -31	1831.368	1831.368	-	1831.368	-	-	1831.368	1831.368	-	-	-	-	-	1831.368	-	-
57-	B6	1864.071	-	1864.071	-	-	-	-	-	-	-	-	-	-	-	-	-
58-	H6 -70	1896.774	1896.774	-	-	-	-	-	-	-	-	-	-	-	-	-	-
59-	H6 -41	1929.477	-	-	-	-	-	-	-	-	-	-	-	-	-	-	-
60-	H6 -12	1962.18	1962.18	1962.18	1962.18	1962.18	1962.18	-	-	-	1962.18	-	1962.18	-	-	1962.18	-
61-	H6 +17	1994.883	-	-	-	-	-	-	-	-	-	-	-	-	-	-	-
62-	H6 +45	2027.586	2027.586	-	-	-	-	-	-	-	-	-	-	-	-	-	-
63-	H6 +73	2060.289	-	2060.289	-	-	-	2060.289	-	2060.289	-	-	-	-	-	-	-
64-	C7	2092.992	2092.992	-	2092.992	-	-	-	2092.992	-	-	-	-	-	-	-	2092.992
65-	C +27	2125.695	-	-	-	2125.695	-	-	-	-	-	-	-	2125.695	-	-	-
66-	C +53	2158.403	2158.398	2158.398	-	-	2158.398	-	-	-	-	2158.398	-	-	-	-	-
67-	C +79	2191.101	-	-	-	-	-	-	-	-	-	-	-	-	-	-	-
68-	C#7 +5	2223.804	2223.804	-	2223.804	-	-	-	-	-	-	-	-	-	-	-	-
69-	C# +30	2256.507	-	2256.507	-	-	-	-	-	-	-	-	-	-	-	-	-
70-	C# +55	2289.210	2289.21	-	-	2289.21	-	2289.21	-	-	2289.21	-	-	-	2289.21	-	-
71-	C# +80	2321.913	-	-	-	-	-	-	-	-	-	-	-	-	-	-	-
72-	D7 +4	2354.616	2354.616	2354.616	2354.616	-	2354.616	-	2354.616	2354.616	-	-	2354.616	-	-	-	-
73-	D +28	2387.319	-	-	-	-	-	-	-	-	-	-	-	-	-	-	-
74-	D +51	2420.022	2420.022	-	-	-	-	-	-	-	-	-	-	-	-	-	-
75-	D +75	2452.725	-	2452.725	-	2452.725	-	-	-	-	-	-	-	-	-	2452.725	-
76-	Es7 -2	2485.428	2485.428	-	2485.428	-	-	-	-	-	-	-	-	-	-	-	-
77-	E7 -80	2518.131	-	-	-	-	-	2518.131	-	-	-	2518.131	-	-	-	-	-
78-	E7 -57	2550.834	2550.834	2550.834	-	-	2550.834	-	-	-	-	-	-	2550.834	-	-	-
79-	E7 -45	2583.537	-	-	-	-	-	-	-	-	-	-	-	-	-	-	-
80-	E7 -14	2616.24	2616.24	-	2616.24	2616.24	-	-	2616.24	-	2616.24	-	-	-	-	-	2616.24
81-	E7 +8	2648.943	-	2648.943	-	-	-	-	-	2648.943	-	-	-	-	-	-	-
82-	E +29	2681.646	2681.646	-	-	-	-	-	-	-	-	-	-	-	-	-	-
83-	E +50	52714.349	-	-	-	-	-	-	-	-	-	-	-	-	-	-	-
84-	E +71	2747.052	2747.052	2747.052	2747.052	-	2747.052	2747.052	-	-	-	-	2747.052	-	2747.052	-	-
85-	F7 -9	2779.755	-	-	-	2779.755	-	-	-	-	-	-	-	-	-	-	-
86-	F7 +12	2812.458	2812.458	-	-	-	-	-	-	-	-	-	-	-	-	-	-
87-	F +32	2845.161	-	2845.161	-	-	-	-	-	-	-	-	-	-	-	-	-
88-	F +51	2877.864	2877.864	-	2877.864	-	-	-	2877.864	-	-	2877.864	-	-	-	-	-
89-	F +71	2910.567	-	-	-	-	-	-	-	-	-	-	-	-	-	-	-
90-	F +90	2943.27	2943.27	2943.27	-	2943.27	2943.27	-	-	2943.27	2943.27	-	-	-	-	2943.27	-
91-	F#7 +9	2975.973	-	-	-	-	-	2975.973	-	-	-	-	-	2975.973	-	-	-
92-	F# +28	3008.676	3008.676	-	3008.676	-	-	-	-	-	-	-	-	-	-	-	-
93-	F# +47	3041.379	-	3041.379	-	-	-	-	-	-	-	-	-	-	-	-	-
94-	F# +66	3074.082	3074.082	-	-	-	-	-	-	-	-	-	-	-	-	-	-
95-	F# +84	3106.785	-	-	-	3106.785	-	-	-	-	-	-	-	-	-	-	-
96-	G7 +02	3139.488	3139.488	3139.488	3139.488	-	3139.488	-	3139.488	-	-	-	3139.488	-	-	-	3139.488
97-	G +20	3172.191	-	-	-	-	-	-	-	-	-	-	-	-	-	-	-
98-	G +38	3204.894	3204.894	-	-	-	-	3204.894	-	-	-	-	-	-	3204.894	-	-
99-	G +55	3237.597	-	3237.597	-	-	-	-	-	3237.597	-	3237.597	-	-	-	-	-
100-	G +73	3270.3	3270.3	-	3270.3	3270	-	-	-	-	3270.3	-	-	-	-	-	-

Table 7: Series of the branch overtones comparable to the main overtone series.

See also the following figures for the first 16 overtones of the branch harmonic series of the C1 overtone tuning system:

Figure 20: Branch harmonic series of the third overtone in C1 main harmonic series.

Figure 21: Branch harmonic series of the fifth overtone in C1 main harmonic series.

Figure 22: Branch harmonic series of the seventh overtone in C1 main harmonic series.

Figure 23: Branch harmonic series of the ninth overtone in C1 main harmonic series.

Figure 24: Branch harmonic series of the thirteenth overtone in C1 main harmonic series.

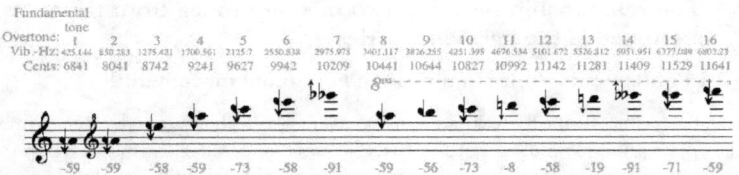

Figure 25: Branch harmonic series of the fifteenth overtone in C1 main harmonic series.

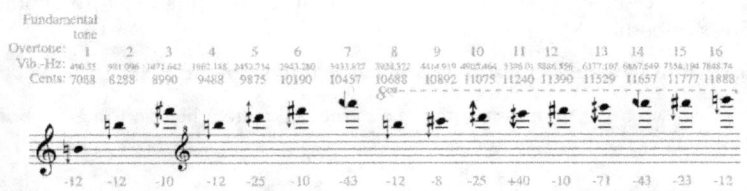

Figure 26: Branch harmonic series of the seventeenth overtone in C1 main harmonic series.

The basic structural properties of the branch harmonic series compared to the main harmonic series are:

- The overtones of the branch series have the frequencies that exist in the overtones of the main-series (see Table 7).
- It is easy to modulate from main-series to one of its branch series, in which case the branch series converts to a main series.
- The intervals of the branch series exist in the main series.
- From a harmonic point of view, the nearest branch series to the fundamental tone of the main harmonic series has more overtones in common with the lower area, nearer the fundamental (see Chapter 5.1.1).

To find an overtone of a branch series concerning the main series the equation $O_v = O_n * O_b$ is used O_v is the overtone number in the main-series.

O_n is the overtone number of the derived-fundamental in the main-series.

O_b is the number of the overtone in the branch series. For example:

The seventh overtone of the thirteenth overtone branch series will exist in the ninety-first overtone of the main harmonic series as shown by:

$O_v = 13*7 = 91$

This shows that the thirteenth overtone of C1 is A4$_{-59cnts}$ (O_n), the seventh overtone (O_b) of the derived fundamental A4$_{-59cnts}$ is 2975.973 Hz. This frequency is the overtone number 91 in the main series, equalling Fis7$_{+9cnts}$ (O_v).

5.2 The relationship between two or more tones from the first 16 overtones of the harmonic series

5.2.1 Fundamental tones in unison in horizontal movement[131]

The harmonic series for two successive tones are fully matched when a musician plays them at the same tone twice in unison. Similar to that is when two or more musicians play the same tone (unison) with instruments that have the same timbre,[132] as both pitches have the same frequency for the fundamental tone and for the rest of the overtones. Thus the overtones for both harmonic series have similar positions, and the movement from one pitch to another flows smoothly.

5.2.2 Fundamental tones in unison vertical movement

Playing two tones in unison at the same time will match the overtones for both harmonic series for these tones.

Figure 27: Shared overtones between two tones are played in unison C1, C1.

---

[131] In general, I use melody to refer the sequence or the horizontal movement of pitched sounds in a musical piece.
[132] Partch 1974, p.68.

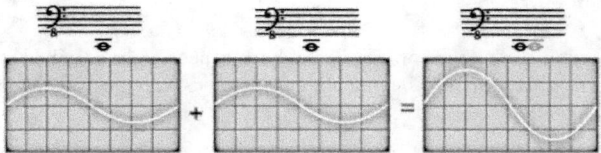

Figure 28: Constructed fundamental tone wave interference from two fundamentals of two tones are played in unison C1, C1.

The relationship between the fundamental tone and the second overtone:

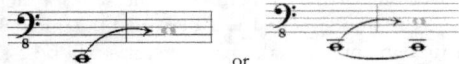

Figure 29: Second possible interval from C1.

If an instrument plays a tone and a second instrument plays the same pitch but an octave higher, the result is an octave between both fundamentals of these tones. Additionally, there is an octave between each overtone from the harmonic series of the second one with its counterpart in the first one. For example: If an instrument plays C4, the first 12 overtones will be C4, C5, G5, C6, E6, G6, B6, C7, D7, E7, F7, G7. If another instrument plays C5, its first six overtones will be C5, C6, G6, C7, E7, and G7. These six overtones of C5 match overtones in C4.

Figure 30: Shared overtone between the main tone C1 and the branch overtone series of the second harmonic accompanying tone C2.

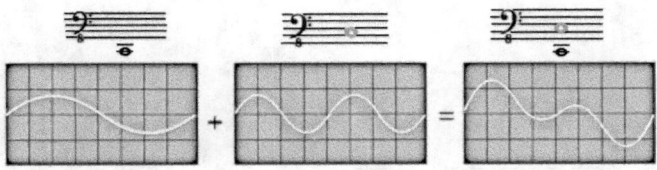

Figure 31: Constructive fundamental tone wave interference for two fundamentals of two tones the second tone plays the frequency of the second overtone of the first tone; one octave higher C1, C2.

The projection of the harmonic series of both tones shows matched overtones and non-matched tones. The matched harmonics can be calculated by the following equation:[133]

$O_v = O_b * 2$

For example, the third overtone in the branch series is the sixth overtone in the main series.

This intense existence for the overtones of branch series in the main series will give the second overtone of the branch harmonic series a high precedence in intervals. As long as its fundamental is a derived fundamental, then the tone will be the main fundamental and the branch series will be a supporter series. For example, if C4 is played by an instrument, then C5 will exist in its overtone series but we hear C4 because it has a higher decibel and because of the resonance of the frequency of C5 which is half of the frequency of C4, making it more dominant.

In this case, the fundamental tone for the main tone will be sub-harmonic for the fundamental of the accompanying-tone. [134]

For example, taking a main series of pitch of C1, and a branch series pitch of C2, the result is all the overtones of C2 match in the main series for C1 (see Figure 21). This makes pitch C2 a supporter to pitch C1, because the fundamental of pitch C2 is the second overtone of the pitch C1.

The relationship between the fundamental tone and the second sub-harmonic tone:

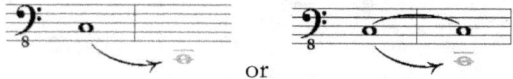

Figure 32: Movement toward the undertone.

---

[133] O_v is the overtone number in the main-series, and O_n is the overtone number of the derived fundamental in the main-series.
[134] Tramo 2003, p.134.

The fundamental tone is the only tone that generates similar pitches in the high-amplitude area of the undertone series (see Figure 32). For example, the correspondent overtones for the pitch C exist in both the overtone series and the undertone series of the harmonic series of tone C4, but the correspondent pitch G_{+2cnts} or pitch $E_{-14cnts}$ is not in the undertone series.

Figure 33: Overtone series and undertone series for C4 fundamental.

Moving from a certain tone to an octave below transitions to the sub-harmonic of the main fundamental tone. This movement supports the new branch series, or the accompanying-tone, as the main harmonic series exists in the branch harmonic series.

For example, if C1 is an accompanying sound for C2, the fundamental of C2 exists in the harmonic series of C1, but not the opposite (see Figure 33).

Figure 34: Shared overtones between the main tone C2 and the branch overtone series of the accompanying tone C1.

5.2.3 The relationship between the fundamental tone and the overtones between the third and the sixteenth overtones

The relationship between the overtones and the fundamental tone is related to the position of the overtones when they are replaced after or before the fundamental. For this reason there are two kinds of movements from a main tone to one of its branch tones or from a branch tone to its main tone.

There are four arguments to explain each of these two cases:

A. The movement from a main tone to a tone of its branch tones in a harmonic series

Observation 1:

The movement from a main tone to a tone of its branch in a harmonic series occurs by playing a tone that has a correspondent overtone that exists in the main harmonic series of the main one.

- The overtones of the new tone will match the overtones of the main harmonic series.
- Thus the melodic movement is smooth; it depends on the number of the overtone which the second musician plays.
- The number of the overtone for the new tone will enrich the main tone harmonic series.

For example, one instrument plays C2 and a second one plays up one octave and a perfect fifth, $G3_{+2cnts}$.

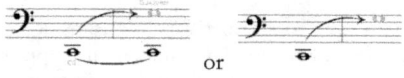

Figure 35: (I, 3) [135]

The fundamental tone of the overtone of the pitch $G3_{+2cnts}$ exists in C2 tone harmonic series as a third overtone (see Figure 12).
The effectiveness of the tone is correspondent to its existence in the harmonic series, so $G3_{+2cnts}$ has more effective consonance than $E4_{-14cnts}$, and in its turn $E4_{-14cnts}$ has more effective consonance than $B4_{-31cnts}$.

Observation 2:

The tone creates a frequency of an overtone in the main tone harmonic series, but the number of this overtone is not an odd number. The frequency of the overtone which the instrument performs follows the equation below:

$O_b = O_{fm} * od * 2N$

O_b is the branch-overtone

O_{fm} is the fundamental-tone of the main-harmonic series

od is an odd overtone number

N is a natural-number, $N \geq 1$

---

[135] The Latin numbers represent the fundamental tone, and the Arabic numbers represent the overtone number in the harmonic series in the nearest octave.

An example is the third overtone of the fundamental tone C2 where the od=3. The first possible overtone is N=1.

$O_b = C2*3*(2*1) = C2*3*2 = C2*6 = O_{G4+2cnts} = G4_{+2cnts}$

Figure 36: $(I, 3^\wedge)^{136}$ tone movement from a main-tone C2 to its sixth branch tone ($G4_{+2cnts}$) in higher octave.

The second possible overtone is N=2

$O_b = C2*3*(2*2) = C2*12 = O_{G5+2cnts} = G5_{+2cnts}$

$G4_{+2cnts}$ is in the harmonic series of tone C2 exactly one octave higher than $G3_{+2cnts}$, which has the odd overtone number of three in the overtone series of the fundamental tone C2. $G3_{+2cnts}$ has a higher amplitude position compared to $G4_{+2cnts}$ or to any other higher $G_{(Pon* 2N)+2cnts}$ overtones.

The higher overtones in a harmonic series are less attracted to the fundamental tone because they are further from the fundamental and they have less amplitude.

It is more difficult to move from $G5_{+2cnts}$ to C0 than to move from $G2_{+2cnts}$ and $G3_{+2cnts}$ to C0, because $G5_{+2cnts}$ is placed further than the two overtones from the fundamental C0, although $G5_{+2cnts}$ exists in another overtone branch series for the main series of C0.

The $G5_{+2cnts}$ overtone with 1569.744Hz frequency exists as:

- The forty-eighth overtone in the main overtone series (*C0*).
- The twenty-fourth overtone in the second branch overtone series (*C1*).
- The sixteenth overtone in the third branch overtone series (*G1*$_{+2cnts}$).
- The twelfth overtone in the fourth branch overtone series (*C2*).
- The eighth overtone in the sixth branch overtone series (*E2*$_{-14cnts}$).
- The sixth overtone in the eighth branch overtone series (*G2*$_{+2cnts}$).
- The fourth overtone in the twelfth branch overtone series (*B2*$_{-31cnts}$).
- The third overtone in the sixteenth branch overtone series (*C3*).

From the above we conclude that in modulation it will have more than one main overtone series.

---

[136] The symbol ($\wedge$) indicates an octave higher. The symbol ($_v$) indicates an octave lower.

In general the higher overtones have less amplitude than the lower ones. For example, as can be seen in the hypnotic spectrogram in Figure 13, C4 or E4+14cnts overtones have less amplitude than G3+2cnts and C3 if we compare them to C2, and so on in order for G4+2cnts, B4-31cnts, C5, etc.

Observation 3:

This observation is based on playing a pitch that has a frequency of no odd overtone number. The frequency of this pitch is an octave or less than the frequency of its odd overtone number in relation to the fundamental of the harmonic series.

The frequency of the overtone which the instrument performs follows this equation:

$$O_b = O_{fm} * od * 1/2^{2N} \quad (N \geq 1)$$

In this case, the branch tone is still subordinate to the main tone. An instrument performs the C2 tone and a second instrument performs the G2+2cnts tone. The G2+2cnts overtone does not exist in the overtones of the fundamental tone C2, but it exists in the overtones of a missed fundamental C1, as C2 is the second overtone and G2+2cnts is the third overtone. C2 has less amplitude compared to C1; consequently, C2 is not a fundamental but the first overtone for the fundamental C1 even though the rest of the overtones of G2+2cnts up to the second overtone exist in the overtones of C2.

The relationship between C2 and the other tones in the M.O.S. will be treated similarly.

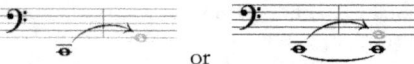

Figure 37: (I, 3v) tone movement from a main-tone C2 to its third branch-tone G2+2cnts within an octave.

In the figure below, D4+4cnts is the eleventh overtone for a missed fundamental C1. C4 will be the eighth overtone in the harmonic series.

C4 is a representative for the C1 overtone, as its overtone series has the same pitch properties. D4+4cnts exists in all *C* pitches, and in case of D4+4cnts and C4, the overtones up to the eighth overtone of D7+4cnts of the harmonic series of D4+4cnts, exist in the overtones of C2.

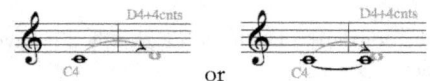

Figure 38: (I, 9) tone movement from a main-tone *C* to its ninth branch-tone D+4cnts within an octave.

Observation 4:

Observation four is similar to observation three in that both describe the relationship between the fundamental tone of the main harmonic series and the missed derived fundamental tone. The reason of the missing overtones in the branch overtone series is that these overtones are placed octaves under their odd number overtones in the main harmonic series of the main tone.

The main tone will be treated as an overtone for a missed fundamental. It has dominance over the branch tone, as the overtones of the branch tone exist in the high area of the harmonic series of the main tone. However, the reverse is not true. The fundamental tone has a higher frequency than the branch tone, the branch tone still has less amplitude than the main tone, and the movement is toward low amplitude.

For example, the C2 overtones and the $G1_{+2cnts}$ overtones do not match directly, so none of them can be a fundamental tone for the other. C2 does not exist in the overtone of $G1_{+2cnts}$, and $G1_{+2cnts}$ does not exist in the overtones of C2. The first common overtone between C2 and $G1_{+2cnts}$ is $G3_{+2cnts}$ which is the third overtone for C2 tone and the fourth overtone for $G1_{+2cnts}$.

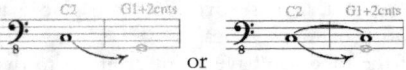

Figure 39: (I,-5) tone down movement from main tone C to a branch-tone $G1_{+2cnts}$.

B. The movement from a branch tone to its main tone

Observation 1:

The movement of the tone in this case is from a branch tone to a tone has the exact frequency of its fundamental tone.

The overtones of the branch tone will match identically with overtones in the mother overtone series. This movement will lead to tonal stability.

For example, the movement of the branch tone $G2_{+2cnts}$ to the main tone C1. $G2_{+2cnts}$ is the third overtone in the harmonic series of the tone C1. This movement counts C1 as a tonic for $G2_{+2cnts}$.[137]

---

[137] Another example can be illustrated as:

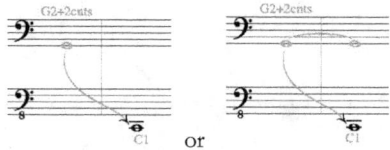

Figure 40: (3, I) tone movement from a branch-tone $G1_{+2cnts}$ to its main-tone C.

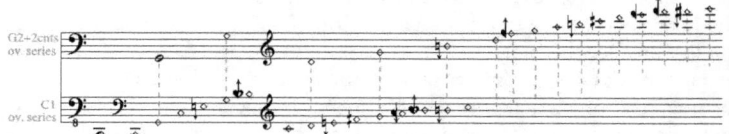

Figure 41: Comparing the overtones in the G3 harmonic series to the overtones in the C1 harmonic series.

Observation 2:

The tone moves down from a branch tone to its main tone in lower octaves. Although the overtones of the branch tone match identically with overtones of the mother overtone series, these overtones are placed in a high overtone number for the mother overtone series.

This movement of the tone will have a similar effect to that in Observation 1 but with higher amplitude as the branch tone moves toward a more stable fundamental.

The example below shows a movement of a branch tone $G4_{+2cnts}$ to its main tone $C2$. $G4_{+2cnts}$ is the third overtone in the harmonic series of the tone $C3$, and the sixth overtone in the harmonic series of the tone $C2$. At the same time, $G4_{+2cnts}$ is the second overtone in the harmonic series of the tone $G3_{+2cnt}$ which is the third overtone in the harmonic series of the tone $C2$. $C2$ represents the second undertone for the fundamental tone $C3$.

Figure 42: (3, I) tone movement from a branch overtone $G1_{+2cnts}$ to a lower main-tone C.

Observation 3:

This observation refers to a tone movement from a branch one to its main tone within an octave.
Many lower overtones from the branch harmonic series which have high amplitude will not be found in the correspondent overtones in the main overtone series. However, there will be matching overtones from the branch harmonic series of the branch tone and the mother harmonic series of the main tone in the high overtones, which have less amplitude. The fundamental tone of the branch tone is derived from odd number overtones in the main harmonic series of the main-tone.

$$O_b = O_f * od * 1/2^{2N} \quad (N \geq 1)$$

The fundamental tone of the branch-series does not exist in the main series (see Figure 20), however, it does exist in the undertones of the fundamental tone series (Figure 33).

This movement is smooth and consonant from the fundamental point of view because a branch tone will move to a main undertone and the main tone will be a branch undertone in a sub-harmonic series for the new main tone.

For example, when there is movement from the branch tone $G1_{+2cnts}$ to the main tone $C1$, the main fundamental from $G1_{+2cnts}$ is $C0$, but $C0$ is an undertone for the fundamental-tone $C1$.[138]

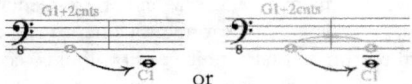

Figure 43: (3, I) tone movement from a branch-tone $G1_{+2cnts}$ to a main tone C within an octave.

The fundamental tone of $G1_{+2cnts}$ does not exist as an overtone in $C1$, but the second overtone $G2_{+2cnts}$ exists also as a third overtone in $C1$, and then the fourth overtone $G3_{+2cnts}$.

---

[138] Another simple example:

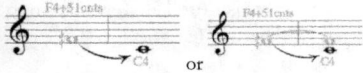

Figure 44: G1$_{+2cnts}$ harmonic series compared to C1 harmonic series.. The fundamental G1$_{+2cnts}$ is not included in the overtones of the main harmonic series of C1.

C1 can also be counted as a third undertone for a sub-harmonic series, in which G2$_{+2cnts}$ is the fundamental tone and G1$_{+2cnts}$ is the second undertone.

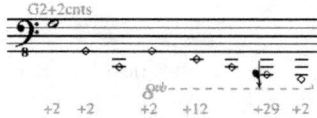

Figure 45: Undertones from G2$_{+2cnts}$ sub-harmonic series.

Observation 4:

The movement of a tone played by an instrument in this observation is upward, from a branch tone to its main tone.
This movement of the tone seems to be more towards an undertone than toward an overtone; the main tone has a higher frequency than the branch tone. In spite of this, it can be an overtone movement for a missed fundamental. Overtones from the branch harmonic series will have correspondent overtones in the mother harmonic series in the higher octaves.
For example, the movement of the branch tone G4$_{+2cnts}$ to the main tone C5, the fourth overtone for the missed fundamental tone C3, and G4$_{+2cnts}$ is the third overtone in the mother harmonic series.

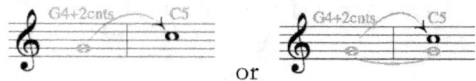

Figure 46: (3, I) tone movement to the third overtone within an octave.

This relationship between G4$_{+2cnts}$ and C5 can be considered differently than the other relationship because C5 is the third undertone for the G6$_{+2cnts}$ sub-harmonic series, and $G4_{+2cnts}$ is the fourth undertone for the same series (see also Figure 33).

In Chapter 5, the relationship between the harmonic series and the sub-harmonic series is demonstrated as the relationship between a dominant and a follower. Moving from a low overtone number to a high overtone number means to move from more consonance to less consonance, and the low overtone numbers have better resonance with the fundamental, but the high overtone numbers have less resonance with the fundamental especially if they are played in the same octave or near octaves. The second reason is that the lower overtone numbers have more dominance in a sound spectrum, as discussed in Chapter 5.1.1. The high overtone numbers follow the lower overtone numbers because the high overtones exist sometimes in the branch-series of the lower overtones, but the opposite is not the case. Thus, the movement from a pitch of a high overtone to a lower one gets more tension, because the second one does not exist in the overtone of the first one.

This method will help in understanding the harmonic structure of this theory. The same idea will be applied to the rest of the overtones.[139]

The above observations about the relationship between the fundamental tone and the third overtone can be applied also to the rest of the 16 overtones and the fundamental tone.

5.3 The relationship between the overtones and the common frequencies in regard to the fundamental tone

In addition to the properties of the branch overtones, the position of the overtones in regard to the fundamental tone will determine the kind of relation between them. The other important aspect is common frequencies for overtones in branch-harmonic series of a certain main overtone series.[140]

Below I will present some important concepts of the relationship between these 16 overtones concerning the fundamental tone.

The first remarkable contact between the overtones of the third branch tone and the overtones of the fifth branch tone of the same harmonic series is the fifteenth overtone in this main harmonic series, which is the fifth overtone in the branch harmonic series of the third overtone. It is also the third overtone in a derived harmonic series of the fifth overtone in the same main harmonic series.

The second common frequency between the overtones of the third branch tone and the overtones of the fifth branch tone of the same harmonic series is the forty-fifth overtone in the main harmonic series, which is the fifteenth

---

[139] See Chapter 5.3.
[140] See Chapter 5.1.3.

overtone in the third branch harmonic series and the ninth overtone in the fifth branch harmonic series.

As an example, according to the branch harmonic series described above in Chapter 5.1.3, the harmonic series of the tone $G2_{+2cnts}$, which represents the third overtone of the main harmonic series of the tone C1, and $E3_{-14cnts}$, which represents the fifth overtone of the main harmonic series of the tone C1, shares C1 the same overtone $H4_{-12cnts}$. In the harmonic series of C1, $H4_{-12cnts}$ is the fifth overtone in the branch harmonic series $G2_{+2cnts}$, and is also the third overtone in the branch harmonic series $E3_{-14cnts}$. The frequency of $H4_{-12cnts}$ is common between $G2_{+2cnts}$ and $E3_{-14cnts}$ branch harmonic series.

The second common frequency between them is $Fis_{-10cnts}$, the fifteenth overtone in $G2_{+2cnts}$ and the ninth overtone in $E3_{-14cnts}$.

The common frequency between $G2_{+2cnts}$ and $E3_{-14cnts}$ can be found by searching for the common multiples between the branch harmonic series of both. These are the overtones 15, 30, 45, and 50 in the main harmonic series and are found through the common multiples of combinations of three and five.

The equation can be written as: $CoM.O. = (O_{b1} * O_{b2}) * N$

- $N \neq 0$ is a natural-number
- CoM.O. is the common multiples overtone
- O_{b1} is the branch overtone no. 1
- O_{b2} is the branch overtone no. 2

The same method can be used to understand the relationship and the common frequencies between the other branch series.

The ninth overtone in a main harmonic series is the third overtone in the branch harmonic series of the third overtone, which strengthens the movement from the third branch harmonic series to the ninth one.

For example, in C1, $D4_{+4cnts}$ is the ninth overtone and also the third overtone in the branch harmonic series of $G2_{+2cnts}$; thus, the branch fundamental for $D4_{+4cnts}$ is $G2_{+2cnts}$. The relationship between C1 and $G2_{+2cnts}$ is similar to the relationship between $G2_{+2cnts}$ and $D4_{+4cnts}$. The complete harmonic series of $D4_{+4cnts}$ exists in the harmonic series of $G2_{+2cnts}$, in addition to the existence of the harmonic series of $D4_{+4cnts}$ in the harmonic series of C1.

A similar relationship is that between the fifth overtone and the seventeenth overtone. In another instance, between the third and fifteenth overtones, the fifteenth is the fifth branch overtone of the third overtone.

5.4 The microtonal harmony within the same harmonic series

5.4.1 The harmonies between two tones

A harmonic structure from a certain harmonic series occurs when two or more tones based on frequencies of overtones that exist in this harmonic series are played. The bond between these tones is based in order according to the distance from the main tone. For example, the movement within the *C* microtonal overtone scale has the following order, depending on the overtone number:

Figure 47: Categorization for the movement of two microtonal harmonics related to the order of overtone numbers of the microtonal overtone scale, starting from the overtones nearer to the fundamental.

The priority of the harmonic movement of the tones in the microtonal overtone scale is based on the movement towards the overtones near from the fundamental.

<u>Case one</u>

Figure 48: Movement from the unison to the other tones in the microtonal overtone scale.

Case two

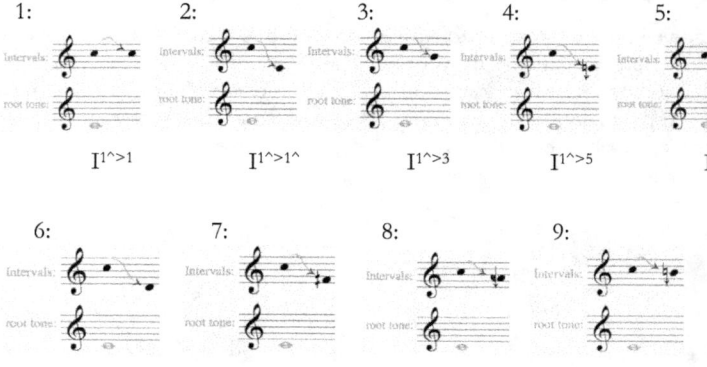

Figure 49: Movement from the second tone in the microtonal overtone scale to the other tones.

Case three

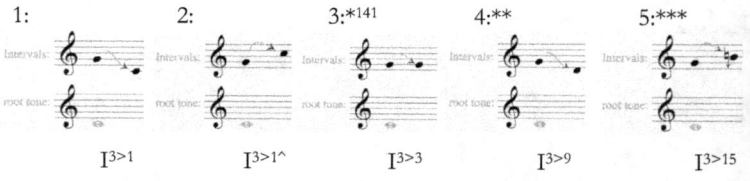

---

[141] (>) A movement from a tone to another;
(*) Unison between two tones which means the overtones of both tones are matched;
(**) Perfect fifth between two tones indicating that the three overtones – the main, the first, the second branch overtones – are matched;
(***) A major third in just intonation between two tones indicating that the three overtones – the main, the first, the second branch overtones – are matched.

Figure 50: Movement from the third tone in the microtonal overtone scale to the other tones.

Case four

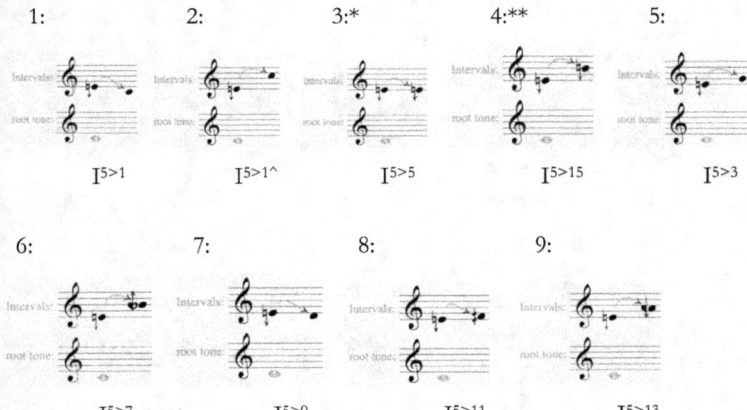

Figure 51: Movement from the fourth tone in the microtonal overtone scale to the other tones.

Further explanations regarding the relationship between overtones and their stability follow in the next chapters.

Case five

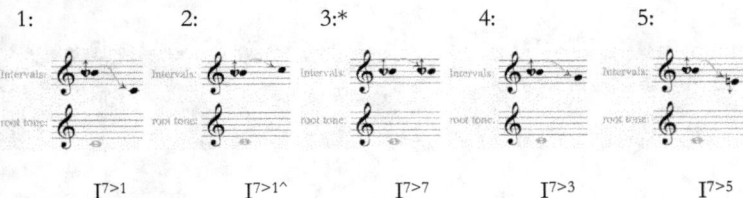

Figure 52: The movement from the fifth tone in the microtonal overtone scale to the other tones.

Case six

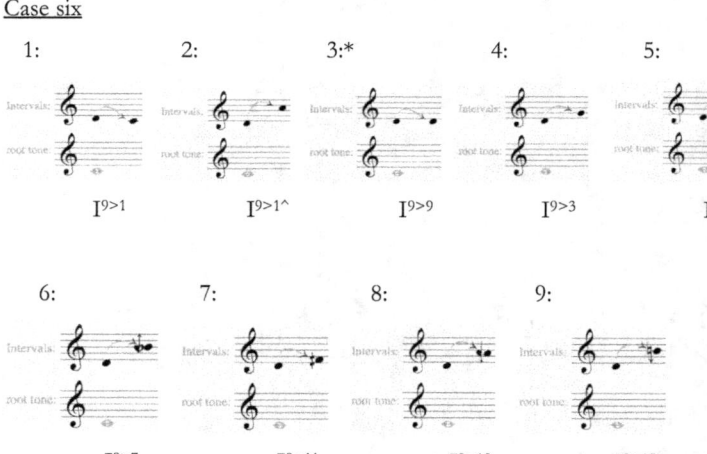

Figure 53: Movement from the sixth tone in the microtonal overtone scale to the other tones.

Case seven

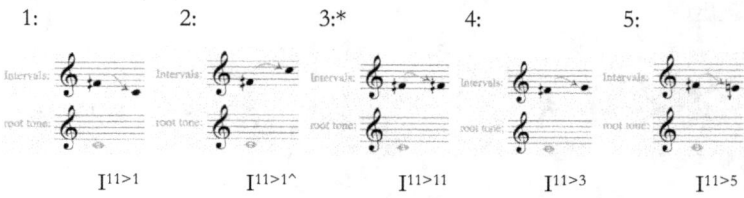

Figure 54: Movement from the seventh tone in the microtonal overtone scale to the other tones.

Case eight

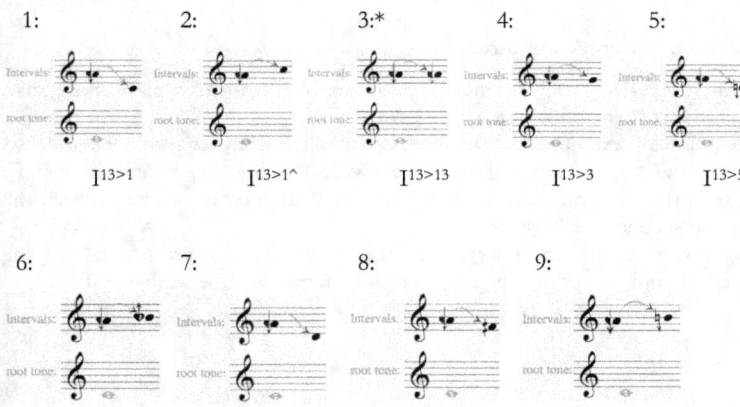

Figure 55: Movement from the eighth tone in the microtonal overtone scale to the other tones.

Case nine

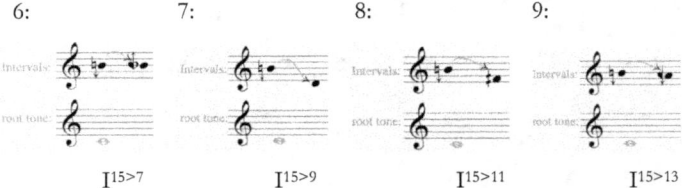

Figure 56: Movement from the ninth tone in the microtonal overtone scale to the other tones.

This two-sound microtonal harmonic movement method forms the principle procedure for the harmonic movement between the other overtone microtonal chords.

5.4.2 The harmonies of three tones

In microtonal overtone harmony one or more instruments plays more than one tone from the same harmonic series.

The following examples are for three tones in harmony. A root tone and two other tones are written within two octaves. There is maximum one octave between the root tone and the first overtone, and another octave between the first and second intervals.

The root tone, the first interval and the second interval are taken from the same harmonic series in which the root tone represents the fundamental.

Example 1:

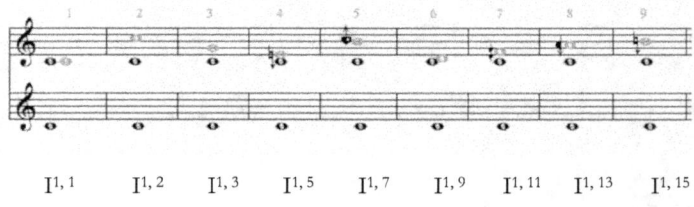

Figure 57: The first interval represents the first overtone. The second interval represents the tones of the overtone scale.

Example 2:

Figure 58: The first interval represents the second overtone. The second interval represents the tones of the overtone scale.

Example 3:

Figure 59: The first interval represents the third overtone. The second interval represents the tones of the overtone scale.

The reasons for this order of numbers are:

- In the first measure, a tone one octave higher than C strengthens the harmonic series of the C. C is also the third undertone in the sub-harmonic of G+2cnts.
- The second measure has two G_{+2cnts} tones, both of which are in the overtones of C. The second interval, G_{+2cnts} ($G6_{+2cnts}$), is the first overtone in the harmonic series of the first interval ($G3_{+2cnts}$).
- In the third measure, both $G3_{+2cnts}$ and $G3_{+2cnts}$ are in the harmonic series of C, but playing the first interval and the second interval in unison strengthen the G_{+2cnts} instead of C.
- In the fourth measure, the overtone D_{+4cnts} is in the harmonic series of C as well as G_{+2cnts}. The overtone D_{+4cnts} is the third overtone of G_{+2cnts}.

- In the fifth measure, the overtone $H_{-12cnts}$ is in the harmonic series of *C* as well as G_{+2cnts}. The overtone $H_{-12cnts}$ is the fifth overtone of G_{+2cnts}.

Example 4:

Figure 60: The first interval represents the fifth overtone. The second interval represents the tones of the overtone scale.

Example 5:

- The first interval represents the seventh overtone:

Figure 61: The first interval represents the seventh overtone. The second interval represents the tones of the overtone scale.

Example 6:

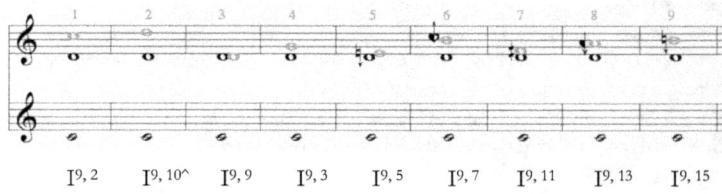

Figure 62: The first interval represents the ninth overtone. The second interval represents the tones of the overtone scale.

Example 7:

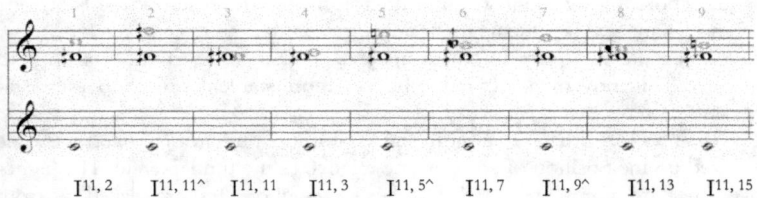

Figure 63: The first interval represents the eleventh overtone. The second interval represents the tones of the overtone scale.

Example 8:

Figure 64: The first interval represents the thirteenth overtone. The second interval represents the tones of the overtone scale.

Example 9:

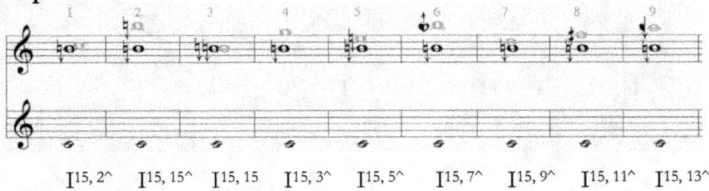

Figure 65: The first interval represents the fifteenth overtone. The second interval represents the tones of the overtone scale.

5.4.3 The harmonic movement of three tones in microtonal overtone scale towards stability

In any chordal movement within a microtonal overtone series, the root tone will not change, as it presents the tone generator and the scale character.[142]

The other intervals form the main material to change the chord from one to another. This movement can either be to a more stable chord or to a less stable one.

The method for moving to a more stable chord in a microtonal overtone scale is based on the position of an overtone relative to the fundamental. The higher overtones are represented by the pitches of the chord and are placed far from the fundamental and have higher frequencies, have the priority to be changed first and moved toward the lower overtones.

The movement of the lower amplitude tone should be toward the higher amplitude.

For example, to move the $I^{11,7}$ chord toward a more stable position, the eleventh overtone should move towards the lower overtone number: 1, 3, 5, 7 or 9. Similarly, the seventh overtone should also move towards the lower overtone number: 1, 3 or 5. The following example is for chord movement within the *C* microtonal overtone scale. The biggest interval between intervals is one octave between the notes.[143]

$I^{11,7}$ $I^{1,1}$ $I^{11,7}$ $I^{1,2}$ $I^{11,7}$ $I^{1,3}$ $I^{11,7}$ $I^{2,3\wedge}$ $I^{11,7}$ $I^{3,2}$

$I^{11,7}$ $I^{3,3\wedge}$ $I^{11,7}$ $I^{3,3}$ $I^{11,7}$ $I^{3,9*}$ $I^{11,7}$ $I^{9,3*}$ $I^{11,7}$ $I^{3,15*}$

---

[142] In some cases, the fundamental tone can be missed; see Figures 26 and 27.
[143] The chords marked with (*) have greater stability.

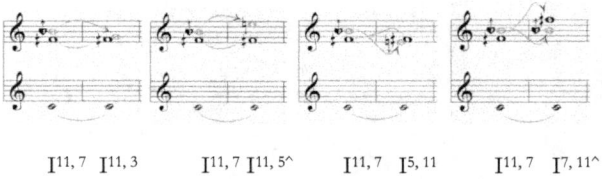

$I^{11,7}\ I^{11,3}$ $I^{11,7}\ I^{11,5\wedge}$ $I^{11,7}\ I^{5,11}$ $I^{11,7}\ I^{7,11\wedge}$

Figure 66: Examples of different tone movement transitions towards stability for three tones in the *C* microtonal overtone scale with a second interval $F_{+51cnts}$.

This previous figures summarize the move from one chord to another, and the same method will be followed among the tones in the chords which have more than three tones in the microtonal overtone scale.

The stability of the harmony in this theory is based mainly on following the category of the overtones of a harmonic series in order; thus, three tones playing the main tone in unison ($I^{1,\,1}$) are evaluated as having high stability for harmony, so that the overtones of these tones will be matched.

The relationship between the intervals plays an important role as has been seen in the chords $I^{3,\,9}$, $I^{9,\,3}$, and $I^{3,\,15}$.

In order for a chord to move smoothly to a more stable position, the movement goes from the weaker to the stronger overtone. For example, the movement from $I^{11,\,7}$ to $I^{5,\,3}$ starts on the eleventh and seventh overtones and descends to the fifth and third overtones.

Cross harmony is possible as far as there are no changes in overtones as in the example bellow:

Figure 67: Similarity in transition.

5.4.4 The harmony of more than three tones

Chords with up to nine microtonal tones can be built in a similar manner to three tone chords.

The example below shows three tones from $I^{5,\,3}$ to which the microtonal overtone scale within one octave for each interval have been added in order to make each a chord with four tones:

Figure 68: Four tones in harmony from the *C* microtonal overtone scale. They are classified according to their position from the fundamental; the fundamental, the first and the second intervals are the same. The third interval is changeable.

In the following example, for five-tone microtonal chords the microtonal overtone scale within one octave for each interval in order has been added to the four chord $^5I^{3,\,1}$:

Figure 69: Five tones in harmony from the *C* microtonal overtone scale. They are classified based on their position from the fundamental. The fundamental, the first, the second and the third intervals are the same. The fourth interval is changeable.

Other chords having more than four tones in a microtonal overtone scale can be written in a similar way.

The harmonic movement towards more stable chords is similar to the example above (Figure 66). Further examples of the nine microtonal chords can better illustrate the idea.

Taking chords chosen at random from a microtonal overtone scale consisting of nine microtones, these chords can be classified in relation to the category of their position from the fundamental as in the following example:

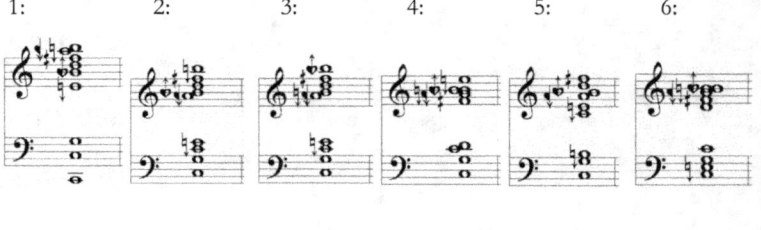

Figure 70: Inversions of nine tones from the *C* microtonal overtone scale classified according to the category of their position from the fundamental.

The reason for the stability in such a category is that:

- Chord Number 1 is more stable than the other chords. The tones are written in order according to the overtone category in a harmonic series from one to sixteen.
- Chord Number 2 has a lower $B_{-31cnts}$ position than the weak overtones positions of 9, 11, and 15. Compared it with chord Number 3, it is seen that $B_{-31cnts}$ has a higher position than the weaker overtones positions of Numbers 9, 11, 13, and 15.
- In chord Number 4, D_{+4cnts} takes the place of $E_{-14cnts}$ in chord Number 3, although $E_{-14cnts}$ has a higher position from the fundamental than D_{+4cnts} as well as the other overtones $B_{-31cnts}$, $F_{+51cnts}$, $A_{-59cnts}$, and $H_{-12cnts}$.
- The main reason for the stability of chords Numbers 7 and 8 is that D_{+4cnts} and G_{+2cnts} are in the correct category in chord number 7; however, in chord number 8, their position is switched. As was previously illustrated (Figure 20), D_{+4cnts} is the third overtone for a main tone G_{+2cnts}.
- For similar reasons, chord Number 10 has a higher $E_{-14cnts}$ than $H_{-12cnts}$ on chord Number 9, but $H_{-12cnts}$ is the third overtone for a main tone $E_{-14cnts}$.

Here is an example of the movement of the nine microtone chord toward more stable chords:

Figure 71: Nine tones represent the microtonal overtone scale tones. They are moving to a high stable chord.

The previous harmonic movement is a high one, where all tones move toward the main tone and its octaves.

Further examples:

Figure 72: Nine tones represent the microtonal overtone-scale tones. They are moving toward stability.

In the previous example, we notice progressive development for nine tones towards their stable chord. In the last chord (Number 6) there are double tones from $E_{-14cnts}$: $E4_{-14cnts}$ and $E5_{-14cnts}$. This strengthens the chord's stability, and the $E_{-14cnts}$ pitch in the chord itself, simplifying the modulation to the $E_{-14cnts}$ overtone microtonal scale. This is an example of modulation technique.[144] From previous examples, we can classify the strength of the chord inversions as follows:

- The weak chords have more tones from the overtones with high odd numbers than from low odd number overtones.
- The strong chords have more tones from the overtones with low odd numbers than from high odd number overtones.

---

[144] Chapter 5.5 and 6.6.

- The tones of the weak chords have no direct relationship between their overtone series.
- The tones of the strong chords can have direct relationships between their overtone series.

The nine tones cluster in the microtonal overtone-scale

The cluster chord for all tones in a microtonal overtone scale within one octave is written:

Figure 73: Cluster for the tones of the *C* microtonal overtone-scale.

5.5 The modulation in the microtonal overtone tuning system

There are many ways to modulate from one microtonal overtone scale to another within the microtonal overtone tuning system. These modulations move from one main tone to another, which means the basic elements of the first tone change. These elements are the frequencies of the overtones belonging to the first main tone.

Modulation happens by strengthening special tones in a microtonal overtone scale which will be the target of the modulation. At the same time, the other tones that have no relationship with the modulating tone are weakened.

There are four ways for modulation:

1- The main branch modulation
2- The branch main modulation
3- The contiguity microtonal harmony scale (branch-branch) modulation
4- The random microtonal overtone scale modulation

1- The main-branch modulation (|–/ or MB):

In this modulation, the microtonal overtone scale of a main pitch modulates to another microtonal overtone scale of a branch pitch by choosing a certain overtone from the first scale and using it as a main tone in the second scale. The fundamental tone of the second one is one of the first 16 overtones of the first, except for the first, second, fourth, eighth, and sixteenth overtones of the main pitch.

For example:

Figure 74: Modulation from the overtone tuning system of *C* to the overtone tuning system of D$_{+4\text{cnts}}$.

2- The branch main modulation (/−| or BM):

In this modulation, the microtonal overtone scale moves to one in which the main tone of the first scale is one of the branch pitches of the second, and the scale of the first is within the overtones of the second (see Table 7). In this instance, the fundamental of the second is a fundamental for both harmonic series. At the same time, the second scale's main tone is an undertone for the fundamental of the first scale.

For example, in the modulation from the E$_{-14\text{cnt}}$ microtonal overtone scale to the *C* microtonal overtone scale, the *C* is not present in the first 16 overtones of the E$_{-14\text{cnt}}$ harmonic series, but the E$_{-14\text{cnts}}$ overtone exists in the overtone tuning system of the *C* as the fifth and tenth overtones. *C* is also the fifth undertone of E$_{-14\text{cnt}}$:

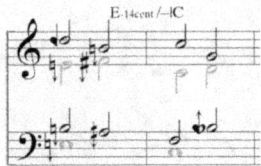

Figure 75: Overtone harmonic movement from E$_{-14\text{cnts}}$ to C$_{+0\text{cnt}}$.

Both the main branch modulation and the branch main modulation can be done directly from E$_{-14\text{cnt}}$ to *C* or from *C* to E$_{-14\text{cnt}}$ without mediator a new microtonal overtone scale without having any linking overtone, as is seen in the previous examples, or they make the change by using one or more linking overtones. The linking tones are shared overtones as they have the same frequencies between two or more harmonic series and support the process of the harmony in the modulation.

3- The contiguous microtonal overtone scale modulation (branch branch modulation) (/–/ or BB):

By using a mutual overtone in two microtonal overtone scales, it is possible to modulate from a microtonal overtone scale of a certain pitch to a new one, where both microtonal overtone scales are neither a branch scale nor a main scale for each other. In other words, the fundamental tone of the first harmonic series does not match the overtone in the first 16 overtones of the second, and the fundamental tone of the second does not match the overtone in the first 16 overtones of the first.

In this case, the new fundamental tone comes through a modulation in a branch mutual overtone which exists in both harmonic series.

The second harmonic series can be a branch harmonic series or a main harmonic series for the first series, but in overtones higher than the first 16 overtones of both harmonic series. Otherwise, both harmonic series have no direct relationship with each other, and the second one is an enharmonic series.[145] When this is the case there are no linking overtones between the two harmonic series.

For example, the C harmonic series and the $E_{-53cnts}$ harmonic series have no direct overtonal relationship, as the fundamental tones of both harmonic series are not present in the first 16 overtones of each other. The modulation process goes through the thirteenth branch-tone, $F_{+51cnts}$, in the first harmonic series, C, which is at the same time the ninth overtone of the second tone, $E_{-53cnts}$:

Figure 76: Overtone harmony modulation from C_{+0cnt} to $E_{-53cnts}$ through the thirteenth overtone.

4- The random microtonal harmony modulation in the microtonal overtone scale (0–0 or OO):

This modulation can be achieved by moving directly to a new harmonic series or to an odd harmonic series without any preparation. The modulation happens without using any of the items from the first harmonic series. The fun-

---

[145] Enharmonic series is a term used for a series of overtones where the fundamental tone has no integer multiples.

damental tones in both harmonic series have no equivalent overtone in the first 16 overtones in the other harmonic series.

For example, while modulating from C microtonal overtone scale to A_{+0cnt} microtonal overtone scale, the overtone series for A_{+0cnt} has no direct relationship with the overtone series of A_{+0cnt}. Additionally, the fundamental C has no duplicate overtone in the harmonic series of A_{+0cnt}, and A_{+0cnt} has also no duplicate overtone in the harmonic series of C:

Figure 77: Random overtone harmony modulation from C_{+0cnt} to A_{+0cnt}.

The examples above were performed by using 1200 cents to an octave. In the compositions that were written to illustrate this theory, the 72-TET and the 24-TET were used to make their results as precise as possible, without complicating the work for musicians and for other composers and theorists who may use or study this theory. In the 72-TET case, the smallest interval in a microtonal overtone scale is 16.7 cents. All intervals, which are equal or less than 16.7 cents, will have the same accidental. For example, all overtones between C_{-8cnts} and C_{+8cnts} are treated as C. In the 24-TET case, the smallest interval in a microtonal overtone scale is 50 cents. All intervals, which are equal or less than 50 cents, will have the same accidental. All overtonal intervals between $C_{-25cnts}$ and $C_{+25cnts}$ are treated as C, and all overtonal intervals between $C_{+26cnts}$ and $C_{+75cnts}$ are treated as $C\sharp$.[146]

5.6 Linking overtones

The linking overtones are used in three methods.

The first method is used to support the fundamental tone of the second scale, where the linking overtone is a branch pitch of the first scale as well as the main pitch of the second scale.

The MB modulation can use more than one linking overtone, if these linking overtones exist in both harmonic series.

For example, D_{+4cnts} overtone is a linking overtone in the modulation between the first microtonal overtone scale C and the second scale of D_{+4cnts}. The ninth

---

[146] See Figure 11.

overtone, D_{+4cnts}, of the first harmonic series, C, is converted into a main tone in the harmonic series of the second:

Figure 78: Overtone harmonic modulation from C_{+0cnt} to D_{+4cnts} through the ninth overtone of C.

The second method creates a smooth modulation from a branch harmonic series to a main harmonic series by using one or more linking overtones. In this case, however, the linking overtone is the main tone of the harmonic series of the first microtonal overtone scale, and it is one of the branch overtones of the modulated microtonal overtone scale.

For example, $E_{-14cnts}$ is the fundamental of the harmonic series of the first microtonal overtone scale. It is also the fifth and the tenth overtone of the harmonic series of the second microtonal overtone-scale, C. $E_{-14cnts}$ is used as a linking overtone in the modulation between both microtonal overtone scales:

Figure 79: Overtone harmonic movement from $E_{-14cnts}$ to C_{+0cnt} through the fundamental and the fifth $E_{-14cnts}$ and the fifteenth $H_{-12cnts}$ overtones.

The third method is based on linking two microtonal overtone scales through their mutual pitches, excluding the main pitches of both scales, so branch overtones linked together help the modulation process. As is illustrated in the previous example, linking between two microtonal overtone scales can happen also through one or more of their overtones.

For example, $E_{-14cnts}$ and $H_{-14cnts}$ are both linking overtones helping in modulation between two microtonal overtone scales. $H_{-14cnts}$ represents the third, sixth, and twelfth overtones of the $E_{-14cnts}$ harmonic series. At the same time it represents the fifteenth overtone of the C harmonic series.

The linking overtone $E_{-14cnts}$ also represents the second, fourth, eighth, and sixteenth overtones of the $E_{-14cnts}$ harmonic series, as well as the fifth and tenth overtones of the C harmonic series. This process takes place while the fundamentals of both harmonic series have no direct link.

Figure 80: Overtone harmonic movement from $E_{-14cnts}$ to C_{+0cnt} through the fundamental and the third overtones.

The example below shows a modulation from the C microtonal overtone scale to G_{+2cnts}, through the overtone $H_{-12cnts}$, where $H_{-12cnts}$ is the fifteenth overtone in the C harmonic series, and the fifth and tenth overtones in the G_{+2cnts} harmonic series:

Figure 81: Overtone harmonic movement from C_{+0cent} to G_{+2cnts} through the fifteenth overtone.

The third method of use for the linking overtone plays a major role in the contiguous microtonal harmony scale modulation.
The main difference between the main branch modulation and the branch main modulation is that main branch modulation goes from a high consonance to a low consonance when it moves from the fundamental tone to an overtone. Conversely, the main tone modulation will gain more harmonic stability while moving from an overtone to its fundamental.

6 The *maqam* system and the overtone series

6.1 Microtonality in Arabic Music

Arabic Music is based on *maqamat*. Microtonal[147] intervals have an important function in *maqam*, although these intervals are not completely fixed. They change from time to time by using *ajnas*.[148] *Ajnas* provide the feeling of modulation to new *maqamat* within the main *maqam* itself.[149]

Many studies have been carried out since the ninth century to give the *maqam* and the music of Islamic period a logical and scientific explanation. The musical study about the *maqam* tuning system was performed by several philosophers and theorists including Abu-l-Hàssan Alí ibn Nafi (Ziryab) (d. ca. 857), Abu Yusuf Ya'qub Al-Kindi (Al-Kindus) (d. ca. 873), 'Ali bin Yahya bin abi Mansur Al-Munajjim (913), Abu Nasr Al-Farabi (d. ca. 950), Abu Ali al-Husayn ibn Abdullah ibn Sina (Avicenna) (d. ca. 1037), and Safi al-Din Al-Urmawi (d. 1294 AD).

With Safi al-Din Al-Urmawi, Arabic music theory reached its summit. Since then, Arabic music has suffered a kind of stagnation, with very little development.[150]

Maqam, as defined in Chapter 2 above, is an Arabic term for mode, scale, or melody. A specific *maqam* is responsible for the feeling or mode of a piece of music, much like a key signature and the relation to the Doctrine of Affections in Western classical art music. The word *maqam* was introduced into the musical language after the thirteenth century to replace the word *naghme*,[151] a tone or a degree. It was used more frequently by theorists between the ninth and thirteenth centuries.

Each *maqam* has a name that refers to its origin, a person's name, or to a special feeling.[152] *Maqamat* are composed of *ajnas*. *Ajnas* play a very important role in the *maqam* structure, which allows musicians to modulate from one *maqam* to another freely.

---

[147] Some musicologists consider *maqamat* like *maqam Ajam*, *Kurd*, *Hijaz*, and *Nahawand* to be equal temperament scales, by comparing them to the Western tuning system. I do not find this correct. For example, *maqam Hijaz*, compared to the major scale, has the third interval slightly lower than the major scale in Western music. This slight difference changes from one country to another or even from one city to another and gives the *maqamat* their characters.

[148] Singular *jins*, plural *ajnas*. Normally two *ajnas* form a *maqam*. These relate to the trichords, tetrachords, and pentachords in Western music.

[149] El Mahdi, Salah. *La musique arabe*. Alphonse Leduc, Paris 1972, pp.45-47.

[150] Maalouf 2002, p.19.

[151] *Nagham* is singular, the plural is *naghamat*.

[152] صلاح الدين، محمد: مفتاح الألحان العربية، مطبعة أحمد مخيمر، القاهرة، ١٩٨٠ Salah ad-Din, Muhammad. *The Key for the Arabic Tunes*. Mkhemer 1980, p.86.

Ajnas can function as trichords, such as *jins Ajam, jins Sika*; tetrachords,[153] such as *jins Rast, jins Bayati*; and pentachords, such as *jins Naua-Athar, jins Mahur*.[154] In many cases the heptatonic scale can present a *maqam*, although theoretically all kinds of other scales can be encountered too, which facilitates the production of immense variability of scales. These scales form the row of *maqam*.

In his book *Kitab Al Musiqa Al Kabir*[155] Al-Farabi explains the process of generating a tone system by applying the Pythagorean mathematical method to define what was called *naghme* (*maqam*) during the Islamic period. Additionally, the circle of fifths was used by most Arabic, Persian and Turkish musicians and theorists to build their tuning systems.[156]

The slight differences in the intervals in the *ajnas* are very important to differentiate one *maqam* from another. The same *maqam* can be used differently in different countries or within the same country. There are three reasons for these differences:

- Due to the different accidental notations in different countries which lead to different tuning systems, the same *maqam* can be used differently. For example, in the Arabic world *qanoon*[157] players use the 24-TET system, but the musicians in Turkey and some musicians in Syria use the 54-TET. The small intervals in the 54-TET give the musicians more freedom to choose the right interval for their *maqam*.

- *Maqam* music is famous for improvisation; many musicians perform the *maqam* as a heritage that does not need to refer to musical theories.

- Between the ninth and the thirteenth centuries when Islamic[158] culture flourished, different theories in tuning systems were written following different mathematical methods.

---

[153] In some theories about the *maqam jins* are defined as tetrachords. صلاح الدين. محمد , p.207.
[154] Al-Humssi 1992, p.113.
See also Farraj, Johnny. *Maqam World*.(http://maqamworld.com/ajnas.html, 2001–03. Accessed 7 Feb. 2016.
[155] Al-Farabi 2009, pp.225–982.
[156] Ashton, Anthony. *Harmonograph*, Wooden Books, Wales, 2003, p.13.
[157] Arabic instrument similar to the *santur* which can perform different equal temperament systems depending on what Urab (Pedals) it has. The 24-TET has 24 Urab in each octave of the instrument.
[158] In the Islamic period, *maqam* music was widely used in most countries under the rule of the Islamic government.

Theoretically speaking, *maqam Ajam* in Arabic music has a scale similar to the major scale in Western tonal music, where the intervals between the tones of each scale are similar either in the 12-TET or in the 24-TET:

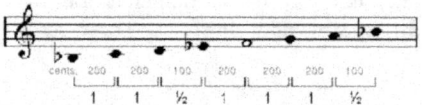

Figure 82: *Maqam Ajam* on B-flat written in 24-TET/ major scale on B-flat written in 12-TET.

This similarity in notation is not realistic in performing traditional Arabic music. *Maqam Ajam* is performed in different ways and it carries different meanings relating to the area that the musician comes from, the instruments used, and the theory adapted in constructing a tuning system.

For example, a similar scale can be written in the same way for the 12-TET and the 24-TET, although it has completely different intervals:

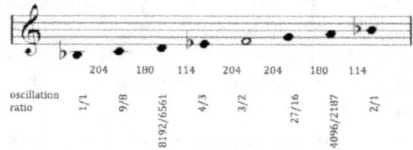

Figure 83: One of al-Urawi heptatonic tuning-system rows written in the 12-TET or in the 24-TET.[159]

The reason behind the similarity in notation and the differentiation in intervals is that each interval is written to the nearest interval in both the tuning systems 12-TET and 24-TET.

If the same scale is written in the 72-TET then it has a different and more realistic notation:

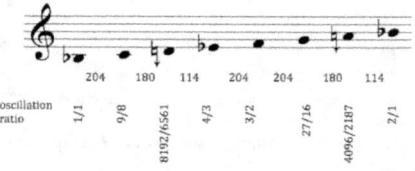

Figure 84: Al-Urawi heptatonic tuning-system rows written in the 72-TET.

---

[159] Maalouf 2002, p.152; Touma 2003, p.22.

In the twentieth century, especially following the Arabic Music Conference in 1932, music theorists including Habib Touma[160] and Salah El Mahdi[161] agreed on adapting the 24-TET as the main tuning system for Arabic music. As far back as the ninth century, theorists like Al-Farabi and Al-Kindi adopted a system very similar to the 24-TET.

Theoretically speaking, although this allows musicians to write down their music, musicians continue to perform *maqamat* in a variety of microtonal intervals. The positions between the pitches and the correspondent intervals are not fixed or limited. Even when musicians move between the pitches of the same *maqam,* they create asymmetric interval melodies, which are responsible for the different musical expressions. This is similar to the difference in the diatonic scales in Western music and the 12-TET. For example, *maqam Rast* can be performed in Syria in a different way than in Turkey, Azerbaijan, or Iran.

6.2 The properties of the *maqam*

Arabic music theories include certain elements that help to explain the properties of the *maqam*. These properties can be summed up as follows:

Maqam rows or the scale of the *maqam* (*al-diuan*)

Al-diuan is composed of the main tones of the *maqam*. These tones are replaced in the main *maqam* rows, which are normally a heptatonic scale, though not always (see Figure 86).[162] Additionally, the second *diuan* should be added to the main *diuan* to give a clear feeling to the *maqam*. These *dauauien*[163] can be counterparts, but not necessarily. An example for the counterpart *dauauien* is *maqam Rast*:

Figure 85: Row of *maqam Rast* and its *dauauin*.

---

[160] Touma 2003, p.24.
[161] See El Mahdi 1972, p.36.
[162] Parfitt, David. *The Oud*. http://www.oud.eclipse.co.uk/index.html, 2001-2016. Accessed 7 Feb. 2016.
[163] Singular is *diuan* and plural is *dauauin*.

An example of *dauauien* that does not function as a counterpart is *maqam Saba*, in which the main *diuan* is different from the rest tones of the *maqam*. It is not a heptatonic scale; it starts on D4 (*qarar*) and ends on C6 (*jauab*) with a sensitive tone F:

Figure 86: Row of *maqam Saba* on D[164] and its *dauauin*.

As mentioned above, this *maqam* is normally written in 24-TET, but it is practically performed with different intervals, as long as the Arabic tuning system is not tempered.[165]
Because of the slight changes of intervals in the different *maqamat*, it is possible to have over 300 *maqamat*. Because modern Arabic music does not use as many intervals, the number of the *maqamat* is diminished to a hundred.[166]
In most parts of this theory the *maqam* is written within an octave, and I call it: The scale of the *maqam*.

The genre of the *maqam* (*ajnas*)

Each simplified row of *maqam* is composed of two or more main groups of notes, each of which can perform melodic material, or *alhan*.[167] The similarities and differences between these groups of notes decide the genre of the *maqam*. The groups of notes called are the *ajnas* which allow modulations between the *maqamat* by passing through a certain *jins* to form a new *maqam*. The *ajnas* reflects the complexities of *maqam* structures.
Within the *maqam*, there are two kinds of *ajnas*: the lower *jins* (*jeze`a*) and the upper *ajnas* which can be connected or separated. The difference between them is that the connected ones have no separating interval with the upper *jins*, but in the unconnected ones the lower-*jins* and the upper *jins* are separated by an interval (see *maqam Rast*, Figure 85).

---

[164] Al-Humssi 1992, p.123. There is another way to write *maqam Saba;* see Parfitt. http://www.oud.eclipse.co.uk/sabaarab.html, 2001-2016. Accessed 7 Feb. 2016, where the *maqam Saba* is written in a slightly different way.
[165] Touma 2003, p.45.
[166] El Mahdi 1972, p.35.
[167] Al-Humssi 1992, p.109.

Genres in practice (*uquod al-maqam*)

There are at least two and maximum five *uquod* in the same row of *maqam*. They are used mainly in the analysis of the *maqam* to explain the relationship between the *ajnas*.

For example, *maqam Saba*, Figure 86, has four *uquod*:

1- *Aqd*[168] one: *Saba*

2- *Aqd* two: *Hijaz*

3- *Aqd* three: *Hijaz*

4- *Aqd four: Jharka*

The Tonic (*Qarar*), Jawab al-maqam, the Dominant (*ghammaz*) and the Hassas Al-maqam

The tonic or the *qarar* is the tone the lower *jins (jeze`a)* starts with. It is in the opposite of the *Jawab*, which is the upper tone of the *maqam*.
The *ghammaz al-maqam* is the second important tone in the *maqam*. It can be its third or fourth tone but in general, it is its fifth tone, but in the example of *maqam Saba* on *D* the *ghammaz* is the third tone (*F*), and in the example of *maqam Rast* on *C* the *ghammaz* is the fifth tone, which is *G*.
Hassas Al-maqam is the minor second interval before the *Jawab*.

Modulation in *maqam*

The modulation in *maqam* music means moving from a certain *maqam* to another by having good understanding of the use of the intervals.
There are two kinds of modulation to go from a *maqam* to another through a common *jins* between both of them, or by moving to a new *maqam*. This new *maqam* has no direct relationship with the main *maqam*, or no common *jins*.[169]

Example of modulation in *maqam* from Arabic music:

Jadaka L-Ghaith is a *muwashah*[170] written by Majdi Al-Aqili in *maqam Huzam*.

---

[168] *Aqd* is the singular of the plural *uquod*.
[169] See Chapter 6.5.
[170] *Muwashah* is an Arabic way of writing songs by using strophic structure and rhythm similar to that were used in Andalusia between the eighth and the fifteenth centuries.

Figure 87: *Ajnas* in *Jadaka L-Ghaith*. Maqam Huzam on E♭.[171]

The *muwashah* starts with the lower *jins (jeze`a) jins Sikah* on E♭ of *maqam Huzam*, then it moves between the other genres *ajnas* of the *maqam*.

---

[171] Fakhri, Sabah. *Jadaka L-Ghaith*. http://www.youtube.com/watch?v=MWyo0R88Oug. Accessed 7 Feb. 2016.

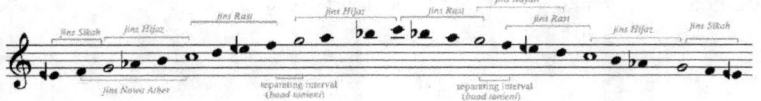

Figure 88: Row of *maqam* Huzam on E♯.

6.3 The *maqamat* in a tuning-system of a harmonic series

The flexibility of the *maqam* is an important property that enables it to adapt to different tuning systems of different cultures and theories. Because of this flexibility, it is possible to have thousands of *maqamat*, for the *maqam* to be different depending on geography, and for the *maqam* to have an entirely new form. For example, there are many *maqamat* that have a special character in the Syrian Desert. These *maqamat* are not found in cities and it is not clear if they are based on a certain tuning system theory or not. One of these *maqamat* was played and sung by Muhammad Sadeq Haded. By analyzing the song we see the following simplified[172] rows of *maqam*:[173]

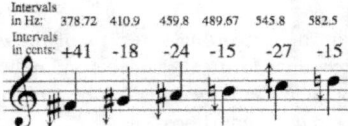

Figure 89: Notes from a row *maqam* is used in the Syrian Desert.

By simplifying the previous row of *maqam* the following system results:

Figure 90: Simplified row *maqam* for the previous example.

---

[172] It is not enough to describe and limit the *maqamat* in just seven pitches. I call the *maqam* written in a heptatonic scale a simplified row of *maqam* or a scale of the *maqam*.
[173] Hadied, Muhammad Sadeq. http://www.youtube.com/watch?v=pRx3NoFnpRM. Accessed 7 Feb. 2016.

Writing the system in 24-TET gives the following *ajnas*:

Figure 91: Possible *ajnas* in the previous simplified row of *maqam* in 24-TET.

This *maqam* has a new order for the *ajnas* which does not exist in the well-known *maqamat*. The nearest maqam to this is *maqam Bastah-Nikar* as it has both *ajnas jins Sikah* and *jins Kurd*:

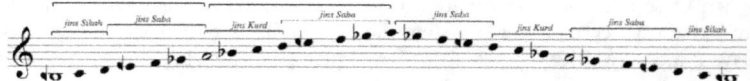

Figure 92: Row of *maqam Bastah-Nikar*.

This flexibility is also in the microtonal intervals of the *maqam*,[174] and its *ajnas*. Flexibility is an open resource for further developments, and for new *maqam* to be created. This flexibility in the *maqam* makes the adaptation of the microtonal overtone scale to the *maqam* world possible.

If the microtonal harmonic tuning system for the C1 harmonic series in the 24-TET, is rewritten[175] the properties of the *maqam* are evident. For example, the following ratios form intervals with in an octave for a tuning system have a certain mode: 8/9, 9/10, 10/11, 11/12, 12/13, 13/14, 14/15, 15/16. See below:

---

[174] Manik, Liberty. *Das Arabische Tonsystem im Mittelalter*. E. J. Brill, Leiden 1969, p.10.
[175] I am using the overtone series written in the 24-TET, which is what Arabic musicians generally use.

The first 16 overtones in a harmonic series written in 24-TET.

Analyzing a row of *maqam* from this tuning system shows that it has the elements of the *maqam*, for example, it has a *diwan* and five *oquod*:

1. *Aqd* one: *jins Ajam* on *C*
2. *Aqd* two: *jins saba* on *F♯*
3. *Aqd* three: *jins Ajam* on *C*
4. *Aqd* four: *jins Rast* on *D*

Figure 93: Row of overtone *maqam* on C.

This *maqam* has a *Ghammaz* on its fifth, *G*, and starts with *jins Ajam*.
There are more examples about this kind of *maqam* in the analysis of the opera *Qadmoos* in Chapter 8.7, in addition to some examples for solo instrument in Chapter 8.3.

6.4 The possible *ajnas* of the *maqamat* in the first four octaves of an overtone

A microtonal overtone scale can have the possible following *ajnas* in the overtone tuning-system:

Overtone *jins*	Correspondent Arabic music *jins*	Overtone *jins*	Correspondent Arabic music *jins*
jins in 72-TET / *jins* in 24-TET	*Jins Ajam/ Jins Jharka*	*jins* in 72-TET / *jins* in 24-TET	
O_v.: 8/9, 9/10	Intv. [176] : 4/4, 4/4	O_v.: 9/10, 10/11	Intv.: 4/4, 3/4

---

[176] Ov.: the overtone number. Intv.: the corresponding interval.

jins in 72-TET / *jins in* 24-TET (notation)		*jins in* 72-TET / *jins in* 24-TET (notation)	
O$_v$.: 10/11, 11/12	Intv.: 3/4, 3/4	O$_v$.: 11/12, 12/13	Intv.: 3/4, 3/4
jins in 72-TET / *jins in* 24-TET (notation)	Jins Awj-Ara	*jins in* 72-TET / *jins in* 24-TET (notation)	
O$_v$.: 11/12, 12/14	Intv.: 3/4, 5/4	O$_v$.: 12/13, 13/14	Intv.: 3/4, 2/4
jins in 72-TET / *jins in* 24-TET (notation)	Jins Awj-Ara	*jins in* 72-TET / *jins in* 24-TET (notation)	
O$_v$.: 12/13, 13/15	Intv.: 3/4, 5/4	O$_v$.: 12/14, 14/15	Intv.: 5/4, 3/4
jins in 72-TET / *jins in* 24-TET (notation)		*jins in* 72-TET / *jins in* 24-TET (notation)	Jins Musta'ar
O$_v$.: 13/14, 14/15	Intv.: 2/4, 3/4	O$_v$.: 13/15, 15/16	Intv.: 5/4, 2/4
jins in 72-TET / *jins in* 24-TET (notation)		*jins in* 72-TET / *jins in* 24-TET (notation)	
O$_v$.: 14/15, 15/9^	Intv.: 3/4, 6/4	O$_v$.: 15/9^, 9^/10^	Intv.: 6/4, 4/4
jins in 72-TET / *jins in* 24-TET (notation)		*jins in* 72-TET / *jins in* 24-TET (notation)	
O$_v$.: 7^/8^, 8^/9^	Intv.: 5/4, 4/4	O$_v$.: 15/16, 8^/9^	Intv.: 2/4, 4/4

jins in 72-TET / *jins in* 24-TET (notation)		*jins in* 72-TET / *jins in* 24-TET (notation)	Jins Rast
O$_v$.: 8/9, 9/10, 10/11. $C_{(8,9,10,11)}$	Intv.: 4/4, 4/4, 3/4	O$_v$.: 9/10, 10/11, 11/12	Intv.: 4/4, 3/4, 3/4

			Jins Saba
O$_v$.: 10/11, 11/12, 12/13	Intv.: 3/4, 3/4, 3/4	O$_v$.: 11/12, 12/13, 13/14	Intv.: 3/4, 3/4, 2/4
O$_v$.: 11/12, 12/13, 13/15 C$_{(11,12,13,15)}$	Intv.: 3/4, 3/4, 5/4	O$_v$.: 12/13, 13/14, 14/15	Intv.: 3/4, 2/4, 3/4
O$_v$.: 12/13, 13/15, 15/16	Intv.: 3/4, 5/4, 2/4	O$_v$.: 13/14, 14/15, 15/16	Intv.: 2/4, 3/4, 2/4
O$_v$.: 13/14, 14/15, 15/16	Intv.: 2/4, 3/4, 6/4	O$_v$.: 13/14, 14/16, 8^/9^	Intv.: 2/4, 5/4, 4/4
O$_v$.: 13/15, 15/16, 8^/9^	Intv.: 5/4, 2/4, 4/4	O$_v$.: 14/15, 15/16, 8^/9^	Intv.: 3/4, 2/4, 4/4
	Jins Kurd		
O$_v$.: 15/16, 8^/9^, 9^/10^	Intv.: 2/4, 4/4, 4/4		

Table 8: Possible *ajnas* in an overtone scale compared to classical Arabic *ajnas*.

This comparison between the *ajnas* of the traditional *maqam* and the *ajnas* of the overtone *maqam* is not completely accurate, as the intervals between both styles can be different. For example, from the table above, in *jins Saba* on F♯, it is more accurate to say that the interval between F♯-G in the traditional *jins Saba* is about 160cents,[177] but the overtone *jins* it is fixed on 151cents,[178] and the interval between G-A♩ in the traditional *jins Saba* is about 140cents. This interval, however, is fixed in the overtone *jins* at 139cents, and the interval between A♩ -H♭ in the traditional *jins Saba* is about 95cents, but it is 128cents in the overtone *jins*.

In this situation, we can deduce two significant arguments.

(1) The *maqam* system is not fixed. As mentioned above, 24-TET is a pragmatic compromise, and musicians can interpret the interval system of a *maqam* in different ways. A composer can define the *maqam* intervals within a certain composition or within a part of a composition by adapting the intervals of the overtone series in one of the above mentioned ways. The composer can then argue that he is still composing within the *maqam* system and that he is interpreting the *maqam* system in a spectral way.

(2) A composer can also argue that he is primarily a spectral composer using the intervals of the overtone series as basic intervals. If he arranges these intervals in a way close to *maqamat*, he uses *maqamat* as a source of inspiration when composing within a spectral and global way of composing and thinking. Any movement between the previous overtone *ajnas* will give a character to the overtone *maqam*. The number of *ajnas* will increase when modulation from an overtone *maqam* to another occurs.[179]

Each of the *ajnas* found in the overtone *maqam* and has no correspondent *jins* in the Arabic *maqamat* possess a special feeling, and can be used individually. These *ajnas* are the overtone *ajnas*, each of which differs from the others by the name of the main overtone and the numbers of the overtones. For example: $C_{(11,12,13,15)}$ [180] is a *jins* in overtone-*maqam* on C that has the following intervals from F♯: 11/12, 12/13, 13/15.

---

[177] In general, the accidental shape ♩ presents the quartertone (50cents), but in Arabic music it is used to refer to the microtones whose range can be approximately between 25cents and 75cents.
[178] From the overtone series (Figure 12) O_{12} - O_{11} = 6702-6551=151cents.
[179] See Chapter 6.6.
[180] It can be written also as a shortcut: $C_{(11-13,15)}$. If the numbers are without interruption the shortcut can be written as $C_{(11,12,13,14)} = C_{(11-14)}$.
A shortcut for *jins*, like $C_{(15,8^\wedge,9^\wedge,10^\wedge)}$ can be written $C_{(15-10^\wedge)}$.

Figure 94: *jins* $C_{(11,12,13,15)}$.

6.5 The possible *ajnas* of the *maqamat* in the chromatic microtonal overtone scale

<u>The chromatic microtonal overtone scale and the *maqam* system</u>

By using the sixteen tones of the C.M.O.S., more *ajnas* can be found. It is of special significance here to consider the theory of overtone amplitude discussed in Chapter 5.1.1 which demonstrates that the amplitude of these overtones is less than the amplitude and consonance of the lower overtones which are closer to the fundamental.

The *maqam* derived from the overtone series is the overtone *maqam* and the *ajnas* found in it are the overtone *ajnas*.

<u>The possible overtone *ajnas* in the C.M.O.S.</u>

It is clear that the C.M.O.S. has more overtone *ajnas* varieties than the M.O.S. As it is illustrated below, *jins Sikah* can start from different overtones:

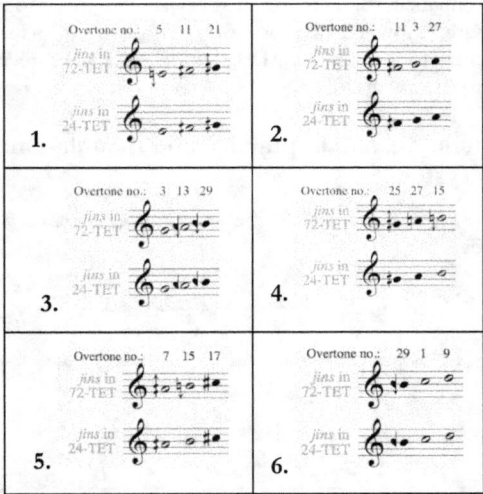

Figure 95: Possible overtone *ajnas* Sikah in a C.M.O.S.

As a *maqam* Sikah it would be more appropriate to start the *jins* Sikah on G♯, as all the tones of *maqam* Sikah are found within the C.M.O.S.:

Figure 96: C.M.O.S-*Sikah*.

The variety of *ajnas* allows a composer of spectral music to choose the relevant overtone *jins* to his idea or the desirable *jins* feeling. For instance, if the composer is searching for a strong tonic then the overtone *jins Sikah* on G, whose tonic is the third overtone in the C.M.O.S. of C is the best. If the composer looks for tones closer to the fourth octave of the harmonic series, overtone *jins Sikah* on A♯ is best, as the tones of this *jins* have the nearest overtones to the fourth octave. Furthermore, if the composer would like to modulate to a different overtone *jins* by starting with the second tone of the same C.M.O.S. for the purpose of enhancing the feeling of the scale, then overtone *jins Sikah* on H♮ (no.6 in Figure 95) would be most appropriate because its second tone, C, is the fundamental tone in the C.M.O.S. of C, giving more stability to the C.M.O.S. than to the *jins* itself.

6.6 The overtone *maqam* in practice and modulation: The "Go in between system"

In the opera *Qadmoos*, Storyteller Scene (Antara), *maqam Sikah* is used in the following melody:

Figure 97: Opera *Qadmoos*, Storyteller Scene (Antara), *maqam Sikah*

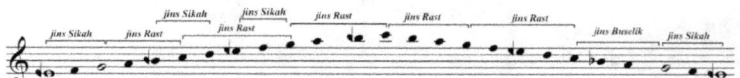

Figure 98: Row *maqam Sikah*.

In the previous example, the tone E♭ is the dominant or the main tone for *maqam Sikah*. If an ostinato is present in the bass, it would be on E♭. By analyzing the overtone series of the basso ostinato, we see that the most suitable overtone series to *maqam Sikah* is that of E♭, although just a few pitches in this *maqam* match the M.O.S. of E♭ and the C.M.O.S. of E♭. E♭ is an important tone as the fundamental tone of the overtone, and as the tonic of the *maqam*. Nonetheless, there are still many important overtones in the E♭ overtone series which exist in *maqam Sikah* in E♭:

Figure 99: Overtone *maqam Sikah* on E♭. White notes illustrate the shared tones with *maqam Sikah* on E♭.

E♭ is the most important pitch when musicians perform *maqam Sikah* in E♭ as it gives stability to the *maqam* and functions as the *qarar*[181] of *maqam Sikah* in E♭. Another important pitch is the fifth, the *ghammaz* of the *maqam*, or dominant, H♭, in the row of the *maqam* a new *jins Sikah* starts.
The eleventh overtone is not as important as the previous ones, but is there to support the overtone of the *maqam*.
The hypothetic spectrum of this M.O.S. can be illustrated as follows:

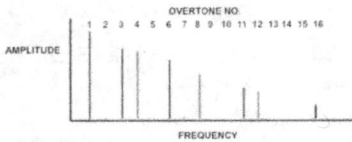

Figure 100: Hypothetic spectrogram illustration for an accord from the *maqam Sikah* on E♭ spectral from.

The possible overtone *ajnas* from C.M.O.S. which can fit into the *maqam* are (B) C.M.O.S., by using the eleventh, third, twenty-seventh, and ninth overtones, in addition to, (F) C.M.O.S. by using the ninth, fifth, eleventh, third, and first overtones, and (H) C.M.O.S. by using the fifth, ninth, seventeenth, and fifteenth overtones:

---

[181] Similar to the tonic in Western music. See Chapter 6.2.

Figure 101: Possible overtone *ajnas* of the C.M.O.S. in the row of *maqam Sikah*.

Thus, the harmony of this overtone *maqam* (see Figure 101) can be written in three main ways:

1- The first is to use the main overtone, which is the *qarar* of the *maqam*. For example, in the example in Figure 102, this way of harmonization can be achieved when main melody of qanoon is played with just the harmony of the cello and the contrabass.

2- The second way is to use an overtone for each *jins* in the *maqam* in addition to the main overtone. For example, in Figure 102, the main M.O.S. harmony of the *maqam Sikah* is from the overtones of E♩ (see Figure 99). The *ajnas* of the *maqam* have different overtone *ajnas* (*jins* B, C.M.O.S., *jins* F, C.M.O.S. and *jins* A,♭ C.M.O.S.), as is illustrated below. Although the shared tones between *maqam sika* and E♩ M.O.S. form the main harmony, the other overtone *jins* are the *maqam ajnas* and the tone supporter.

3- The third way is to write different M.O.S. harmony to each tone in the *maqam*, where each of these tones exists in a different M.O.S. This is similar to the last chord in Figure 102 in which the harmony is fully written in main E♩ M.O.S.

In the example bellow, I illustrate the Storyteller Scene from opera Qadmoos. *Antara, The Storyteller Starts His Game:*

Figure 102: *Qadmoos*, Storyteller Scene (*Antara, The Storyteller Starts His Game*), bars 1-2. *Maqam Sikah* is used for the melody and the overtone *ajnas* for the harmony. The numbers illustrate the overtone numbers in their C.M.O.S.

Similarly to the classical *maqam* properties in intervals, the intervals in the overtone *maqam* also are not totally fixed, and the movement between the intervals follows the overtone movement theory discussed in Chapter 5. The change in an interval is small; less than 25 cents, or between a minor second (>75,<25) and a quartertone (>25,<75).

In this research, I use two kinds of overtone *maqam* in harmony and melody:

1. The first is the classical Arabic *maqam* discussed seen above. In the classical Arabic *maqam*, it is necessary to add *ajnas* from different overtone series, while the main overtone series performs just a few overtones, mainly the fundamental tone.

2. The second overtone *maqam* is the *maqam* that has no direct relation to the classical *maqam*; however, it has a direct relationship with only one harmonic series and has its tones from the first 16 overtones within a harmonic series M.O.S. It can also be derived from the C.M.O.S. of a harmonic series.

<u>The overtone *maqam* in melody</u>

Performing music by moving between the pitches of an overtone series with respect to the *maqam* properties gives the feeling of a certain mode; the overtone *maqam*. Any melody or harmony played within this *maqam* will be dominated by this mode.

Figure 103: *Qadmoos*, Storyteller Scene (*Antara*): melody in E M.O.S.

<u>The overtone *maqam* modulations</u>

The *ajnas*, as the main elements for modulation in the *maqam*, will be used in the overtone *maqam* to modulate from one overtone *maqam* to another. In this case the overtone *maqam* will keep its mood without breaking any rules relating to the overtones or *maqam*. Otherwise it is just overtone music, or *maqam* music.

Playing two tones could be enough to define a *jins* in an overtone *maqam*. These tones are ascribed to the lower region of the nearest overtone *maqam*. For example,[182] playing *A* and then *H*♩ shows that the nearest overtone series for both tones is *D*, where *A* is the third overtone and *H*♩ represents the thir-

---

[182] These examples are written in 24-TET.

teenth overtone. This *jins* of this overtone *maqam* can be written within a *jins* in many ways; it can be written like this: F#, G♯, A, H♮, $D_{(10-13)}$ / $D_{(11-14)}$ or $D_{(12-15)}$.

Another example takes the pitches G and D♯ and groups them with the suitable *jins* in one group of four pitches: D♯ -!-!-G.[183] This interval is equal to 9/7 and can be found in a lower position from the fundamental, between the seventh and the ninth overtone of an overtone series. This series belongs to the overtone-*maqam* on F: D♯, E, F, G /$F_{(14-2^\wedge)}$.

The modulations between different overtones *aqamat* based on different main tones lead to a multi-tone system as there is no limit for the use of different microtones in the modulations. Whenever there is movement from a specific overtone *maqam* of a main-tone to another, new microtones belonging to this new main tone appear. By modulating to a new overtone *maqam* of a branch tone from the previous overtone *maqam*, there is another new overtone *maqam*. Its intervals are similar to previous overtone *maqam* but its microtonal pitches are different, and for this reason using an equal temperament tuning system puts a limit to the multi-tone system.

Another way can be followed to find a relationship in melody and harmony between the overtone *maqam* and the M.O.S.

<u>The overtone *maqam* in harmony</u>

The harmony of the overtone *maqam* is made from the combination of the overtone system and the *maqam*, and follows these two conditions: the overtone system conditions as explained in Chapter 5; and the *maqam* conditions, especially by maintaining the melody movement as explained in previous parts of this chapter.

One of the remarkable examples of the harmony of the overtone *maqam* is the Sygyt style of the Tuvan Khoomei. An example of this kind of singing is the "Huun Huur Tu" performed at the Philadelphia Folk Festival, August 2006.[184]

---

[183] From D♯ to E is 3/4, from E to F is 2/4 and from F to G 4/4. 3/4+ 2/4+4/4=9/4.
[184] "Huun Huur Tu" at the Philadelphia Folk Festival, August 2006.
http://www.youtube.com/watch?v=RxK4pQgVvfg&feature=kp. Accessed 7 Feb. 2016.

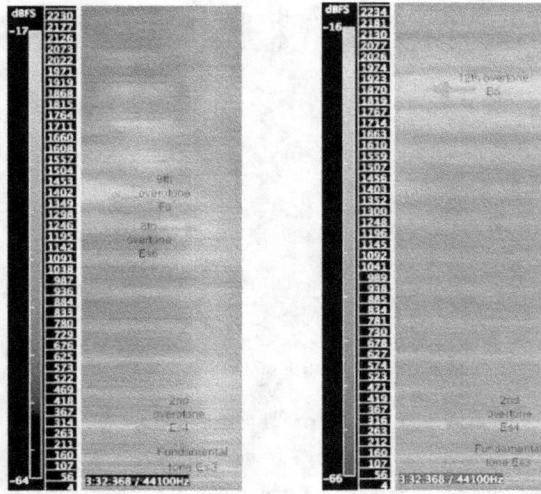

Figure 104: Chosen location for sound spectrogram of the Sygyt style solo singing at the "Huun Huur Tu" at the Philadelphia Folk Festival, August 2006.

The singer uses an overtone tuning system while singing the fundamental tone:[185]

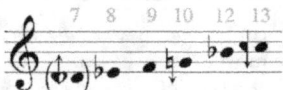

Figure 105: Overtone pitches that the singer of the Sygyt style of the Tuvan Khoomei uses in his overtone song written in the 72-TET.

By using the previous tuning system the music obtains a mode has both properties: the overtone tuning system and the traditional Mongolian music throughout the performance of the piece.

The remarkable notification feature of his singing is that he starts by the seventh overtone Des. He played this seventh overtone as a normal tone but three octaves lower than its normal harmonic position to move then to the fundamental pitch Es. Later in the song the singer concentrates on the ninth overtone F, then the twelfth overtone B. He sings the overtones between the

---

[185] The software used in this analysis was Sonic Visualiser.

seventh and the thirteenth except for the eleventh overtone. The ending tone of his singing is the fundamental pitch, the eighth overtone *Es6*:

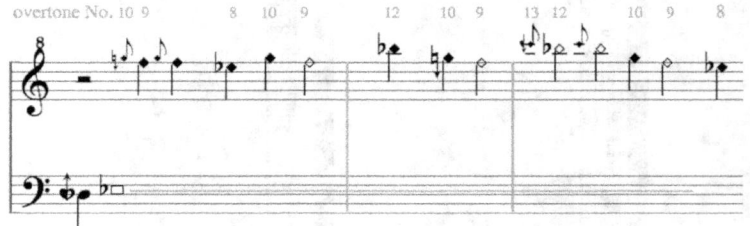

Figure 106: Melodies from the analysis of the Sygyt style singer of the Tuvan Khoomei "Huun Huur Tu" at the Philadelphia Folk Festival, August 2006.

There are three ways to write the harmony of the overtone *maqam* making various simultaneous kinds of modulation.

A. Mono-overtone *maqam* harmony

This starts with one of the pitches of the fundamental tone and creates the mood of the overtone series by switching between its overtone *ajnas*.

<u>A different case in writing the mono-overtone *maqam* harmony</u>

Starting with a main tone from a *jins* in a *maqam* which exists also in an overtone series, this harmonic movement is based on the relationship between the main and the branch overtone series where both form the *ajnas* of a certain *maqam*. For example, in case of *maqam Rast* on *C*, there are two *ajnas* on *C* (*C*, *D*, *E♩*, *F*) and on *G* (*G*, *A*, *H♩*, *C*). Both *ajnas* exist in different overtone series. The first *jins Rast* on *C* exists in the *B* overtone series and the second *jins Rast*, on the *ghammaz al-maqam G*, exists in the *F* overtone series. *F*, however, is the third overtone in the harmonic series of *B*, meaning the overtone series of *F* exists within the overtone series of *B*, and *F* is a branch overtone series of *B*. Thus, there are parallel tones between both *ajnas C* facing *G*, *D* facing *A*, *E♩* facing *H♩*, and *F* facing *C*.

The dominating mode in this case is the harmonic series of the main-tone, while the branch mode is the mode of the second *jins*.

Figure 107: Two tones harmony for *maqam Rast* written in 24-TET.

Figure 108: Four tones harmony for the overtone *maqam Rast* rewritten in 72-TET. The fundamentals B and G_{+2cnts} are missing.

Figure 109: Four tones harmony for *maqam Rast* written in 24-TET.

Figure 110: The above *maqam Rast* four tones overtone harmony rewritten in 72-TET. The fundamentals B and G_{+2cnts} are missing.

Figure 111: Storyteller Scene, *Antara: The holy war*, bar. 158. A random harmonic movement for an overtone *maqam* within a C.M.O.S.

B. Mono-*maqam* multi-overtones harmony

In this case there are different overtone *ajnas*, each of which is based on a classical *maqam jins*. The example in Figure **102** illustrates a melody written in *maqam Sikah*. The main harmony of this melody is written according to the overtone series of E♮. A parallel movement for the harmony is also possible.

This parallel overtone harmonic movement can be achieved by modulating the horizontal line, which is written in advance as a classical *maqam* or as an overtone *maqam* in each vertical line. The intervals between the tones of each vertical line of these parallel *maqamat* or *ajnas* are overtone intervals.

The vertical tones of the overtone *maqam* harmony are responsible for generating parallel melodies:

Figure 112: Parallel harmony movement for three different *qararat*[186] of *maqam* Bayati.[187]

C. Multi-*maqam* multi-overtone harmony:

It is possible to go further with the harmony of the overtone *maqam* to make it more colourful with different overtone *maqamat*, whereby both overtone tuning systems and *maqamat* form two horizontal and vertical diminutions.

Random harmonic movement

This kind of harmony is often formed by using more than one overtone and more than one *jins or maqam* horizontally and vertically. This combination between overtones and *maqamat* changes over time. The horizontal movement is the main producer of the change to different *maqamat* and overtones, which affects the vertical function of the harmony.

---

[186] *Qararat* is the plural of *Qarar*, the tonic of the scale in Western music.
[187] I composed *Flowers Ceremony of sadness* in 2011 in 24-TET.

7 Musical instruments and special microtonal music

Performing the overtone *maqam* by using Western and Arabic musical instruments creates difficulties due to the methods used in manufacturing the instruments. Some instruments are designed to perform in 12-TET, or in the case of the Arabic qanoon, in 24-36-54-TET. Some techniques should be used to compose and perform the microtones:

Woodwind instruments: Performing microtones is easier with open-hole woodwind instruments than those with closed keys. A wide range of possible microtones is possible, produced by overblowing. [188] Choosing different positions for fingers for open- and closed-hole woodwind instruments can lead to some microtones that cannot be produced with the normal fingering.

Brass instruments: All brass instruments produce pitches from the overtone series by overblowing.[189] Some instruments, such as the trombone, perform microtones easily, while others, such as the trumpet and tuba, have greater difficulty in producing overtones. Although it is difficult to play microtones on trumpet and tuba, it is possible by coordinate the valves pressing blowing. It is possible to obtain microtones from the French horn by inserting the hand in a certain way inside of its bell.

Percussion instruments: Normally these are non-harmonic instruments, although some composers, such as Harry Partch, designed microtonal percussion instruments.

Keyboard instruments: Some instruments were designed to perform microtonal music like the Haba piano. Recent research by music theorists and musical instrument designers including Dolores Catherino, Robert Faulkrod, Norman Henry, Ivor Darreg, and Harry Partch concerning the construction of keyboards able to play music in microtonal scales has shown the different tuning systems which composers write special composition for these keyboard instruments.[190] The Fluid Piano designed by the composer Geoff Smith is the most recent example of a keyboard instrument designed to play microtonal music.[191]

String instruments: It is quite simple to perform microtones on stringed instruments.

---

[188] See Bartolozzi 1967. Bartolozzi collected and discovered new techniques for woodwind instruments concerning the tone in different aspects: monophonic, multi-phonic, and combined them for multi-phonic possibilities of special effects and microtones.
See also Adler, Samuel. *The Study of Orchestration*, W.W.Norton & Company Inc., New York 2002, p.166.
[189] Sethares 2005, p.29.
[190] Hugh, Davies, *Microtonal instruments.*, *The New Grove Dictionary of Music and Musicians*. 2nd ed., vol.16, Macmillan Publishers Limited, London 2001, pp. 617–623.
[191] Mills, Merope. "Composer reinvents the piano." *The Guardian*. 1 Feb. 2003, http://www.theguardian.com/uk/2003/feb/01/arts.artsnews1. Accessed . 7 Feb. 2016.

8 Analysis of my compositions in relation to the theory of spectral microtonal harmony

8.1 *Minus One Beautiful One* for cello

The main object for writing this piece was to show the beauty and the behaviour of a certain microtonal interval in a composition, and to prove that each interval has its own mood and function. In this piece, I mixed two equal tempered systems: the 72-tone tempered system which is written to play the sixths of the interval in the 72-tone tuning system, and the 12-tone tempered tuning system, which create the target system, a mixture of an interval from 12-TET with the first interval of the 72-tone tuning system.[192] The desired feeling in the melody is the 12-TET, minus or plus one-sixth of the interval of the semitone. The audience will enjoy the feeling of these intervals, which have their own beauty, and they will not be disturbed by the dissonance of the melody.

This way of dealing with the intervals in a tuning system is similar to the method used to deal with the main tone temperament theory, though it differs in some ways. This system has no certain scale or fixed pitches; it can always be changed. In addition, the interval of the sixth of a small second about 16.66 cents of the small second is equal to the ratio 383:365 which is equal to 83.33cents. The intervals in the piece are as follows: 12-TET (interval) ± 383:365.

Figure 113: *Minus One Beautiful One* for Cello.

This fragment of the piece *Minus One Beautiful One* in Figure 113 shows a part of the melody.

The formula is: [(the main interval) - or + (one of the12-TET intervals) - or + (1/6)], or [(the main interval) - or + (one of the12-TET intervals) - or + (16.7 cents)]:

---

[192] In other word, it can be written as $T2=T1\pm[(N*100)\pm(100/6)]$, that T2 in cents is the result of the previous tone added or subtract from the next 12-TET tone (N*100), N is a natural number. For example: if $T1=D1=200_{cnt}$ and $N=4$ The next tone could be $T2=200+[(4*100)-(100/6)]\approx 200+383,333=583,333_{cnt}$. (N*100) represents the 12-TET and (100/6) represents the 72-tuning system).

H
$[(H)-(1/2)-(1/6)] = A\sharp$
$[(A\sharp)+(3)+(1/6)] = E\sharp$
$[(E\sharp)-(7/2)+(1/6)] = A\natural$
$[(A\natural)-(1/2)-(1/6)] = G\sharp$.

Using the above formula, it is possible to move between microtonal notes without breaking the feeling of the 12-tone tempered system while maintaining the feeling of 12-TET semitone minus or plus one-sixth.

The major second interval is 200-16.7=183.3 cents, instead of 200 cents, which is a major second in the interval between the overtone numbers eight and nine, or in major third between the overtone numbers three and four.

This technique is used for building melodies in the opera *Qadmoos* and is also used to switch between spectrums without breaking the musical structure where there are small differences per cents in intervals. For example, the $C_{+190cnts}$ will be D.

One of the other techniques used in this piece is the microtonal movement, similar to glissando captured in melodies:

Figure 114: Part of the piece *Minus One Beautiful One*, in microtonal movements between D, A and $F\sharp$, $C\sharp$.

In this part, both tones of the perfect fifth are moving a major second plus a sixtieth of a semitone up till they reach the quartertones of both:

The first perfect fifth: X^{193} moves to $X+1/4$: quartertone.

And the second perfect fifth:

$X+2+(1/4)$ moves to $X+2+(1/4)+(1/4) = X+2+(1/2)$: semitone.

---

[193] X is the first fifth.

This melody of microtonal intervals can be classified as a free microtonal system, and it can be compared to the system that Julian Carrillo discusses in his theory *el sonido-13*. He uses the perfect fifth to build the scale where he found that each pure fifth has a new fifth. After a sequence of 12 fifths, there will be a new pitch which he calls the sound-13.[194] This sequence of fifths leads to infinite divisions in an octave. Likewise, by adding or subtracting a sixtieth of a semitone interval (100/6=16.66 cent) to a 12-TET interval, there will be also infinite divisions in an octave: [(a 12-TET interval)± [(sixtieth of a semitone interval)] ±[(a 12-TET interval)± [(sixtieth of a semitone interval).

For example: $C= 200+16.66 =216.66$ cents $= D_{+16.666cnts}$

$D_{+16.66cnts} + 16.66 =216.66+[(300)+(16.66)]=533.33$ cents $= F_{+533.333cnts}$

8.2 *Sudoku* for cello

The reason behind writing this piece was to prove that an aesthetic feeling of pleasure can be achieved by using numbers in a mathematical game to construct a microtonal musical piece. This experiment allowed me to guide the mathematical, microtonal movement and the aesthetic aspect in my theory of spectral music.

Additional reasons for composing the piece are:

- The development of a new mathematical musical idea.
- The use of the Sudoku multi-tuning system idea in other compositions such as the opera *Qadmoos* where the *maqam* system and C.M.O.S. are already present.
- The creation of a piece with a logical mathematical relationship to its dynamics, duration, and intervals.
- The addition of performance practice guidance such crescendo, diminuedo, glissando. Although this sort of guidance is standard in tradition compositions, this piece is written on a mathematical idea. There is no composition; just the conversion of numbers into notes. The composer`s job comes at the end to give the work a musical and a human aesthetic by adding the performance practice guidance.

Sudoku is a mathematical game built on nine lines. Each line has nine squares with numerals from one to nine to be written each time in a different order, provided that no number can be repeated twice horizontally or vertically. The columns and rows must always have the same sum. There are also nine matrices, each composed of nine numerals, which obey the previous conditions.

---

[194] Carrillo, Julian. *Julian Carillo y el Sonido 13, Revolucion del Sonido 13*, http://www.sonido13.com/sonido13.html, 11.07.2009 Accessed 7 Feb. 2016.

Sudoku is built on a logarithmic scale consisting of nine pitches, with each main pitch divided into nine logarithmic branch fraction pitches, resulting in 81 intervals.
The scale, fractions, and the duration of the piece are also built by using the exponential equation.

<u>What is the relationship between Sudoku and music?</u>

Sudoku is a game with strict rules that affect the feelings of the player. In the beginning, the player will doubt his or her ability to solve the problems. Once involved, the player becomes interested; however, solving the problems and winning is not easy.

Figure 115: Transforming three matrices to musical pitches.

The line and the first nine notes of the Sudoku take about 18.5 seconds to be performed.
Time is divided logarithmically between one-ninth of the second to nine seconds.
In the figure above I have started from left to right and from top to bottom: the main pitch, the fraction of the pitch and the dynamic, the duration of the pitch=5, 6, 1.
The first number of the first line of the first matrix refers to the octave:

1 to 3: The first octave in cello which starts by C^2.

4 to 5: The first octave in cello which starts by C^3.

6 to 9: The first octave in cello which starts by C^4.

Figure 116: Illustration of the main nine divisions of the 81-TET *Sudoku* scale, in addition to the first division between the main pitches one and two on the cello.

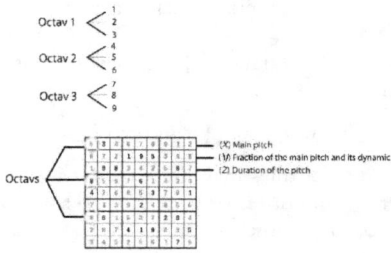

Figure 117: Illustration of *Sudoku* game with the musical background.

Thus, $F^2_{+33\text{ cents}} = T_5$ refers to the main tone in the second octave of the cello between $C^2 = T_1$ and $C^3 = T_9$ The main tones in this octave are calculated as follows: $T_n = 130.812 * 2^{((n-1)/9)}$ (n is a natural-number, , $0 < n \leq 9$)

Its distributive is written: $(T_n, T_{n,bn})$.

T_n is a main tone and $T_{n,bn}$ is a branch tone $(_{bn})$ to a main tone $(_n)$.

$T_{1,1} = 130.812$ Hz $= (1, 1) = 4800$cents $= C^2$

$T_{2,1} = 141.284$ Hz $= (2, 1) = 4933$cents $= C^2\#_{+33\text{ cents}}$

$T_{3,1} = 152.596$ Hz $= (3, 1) = 5067$cents $= D^2_{+67\text{ cents}}$

$T_{4,1} = 164.813$ Hz $= (4, 1) = 5200$cents $= E^2$

$T_{5,1} = 178.008$ Hz $= (5, 1) = 5333$cents $= F^2_{+33\text{ cents}}$

$T_{6,1} = 192.259$ Hz $= (6, 1) = 5467$cents $= F^2\#_{+67\text{ cents}}$

$T_{7,1} = 207.651$ Hz $= (7, 1) = 5600$cents $= G^2\#$

$T_{8,1} = 224.275$ Hz $= (8, 1) = 5733$cents $= A^2_{+33\text{ cents}}$

$T_{9,1} = 242.231$ Hz $= (8, 1) = 5867$cents $= A^2\#_{+67\text{ cents}}$

$T_{9+1,1} = T_1^{+8}{}_{,1}$ 261.624 Hz $= (9, 1) = 6000$cents $= C^3$ [195]

---

[195] $T_{9+1,1} = T_1^{+8}{}_{,1} = T_1$ octave higher

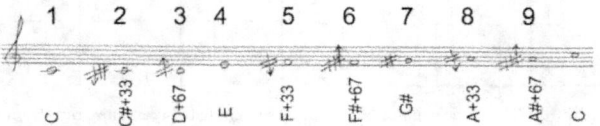

Figure 118: Nine principle pitches of *Sudoku*/ 9-TET scale.

The nine branch intervals in each main tone are calculated as follows: $T_{n,bn}$ =$130.812*2^{\{[(n-1)+((bn-1)/9)]/9\}}$

The first pitch (5, 6) is between (5, 1) and (6, 1):

$T_{5,1}$ 178.008 Hz= (5, 1) = 5333 cents= $F^2_{+33cents}$

$T_{5,2}$ 179.537 Hz= (5, 2) = 5348 cents= $F^2_{+48cents}$

$T_{5,3}$ 181.08 Hz= (5, 3) = 5362 cents= $F^2_{+62cents}$

$T_{5,4}$ 182.637 Hz= (5, 4) = 5378 cents= $F^2\#_{-22cents}$

$T_{5,5}$ 184.206 Hz= (5, 5) = 5393 cents= $F^2\#_{-7cents}$

$T_{5,6}$ 185.789 Hz= (5, 6) = 5407 cents= $F^2\#_{+7cents}$

$T_{5,7}$ 187.386 Hz= (5, 7) = 5422 cents= $F^2\#_{+22cents}$

$T_{5,8}$ 188.996 Hz= (5, 8) = 5437 cents= $F^2\#_{+37cents}$

$T_{5,9}$ 190.62 Hz= (5, 9) = 5452 cents= $F^2\#_{+52cents}$

$T_{5,9+1}$ = $T_{6,1}$ 192.259 Hz= (6, 1) = 5467 cents= $F^2\#_{+67cents}$

Figure 119: Illustration of the first nine divisions of the 81-TET *Sudoku* scale on the cello.

Insofar as *Sudoku* has a logical way to be solved, the lines can be switched or rotated; the same solution will result so there are thousands of possibilities. One of the possibilities is to switch between the lines. The first will be the second, second will be the third and the third will be the first. The music will change as it does in the following example:

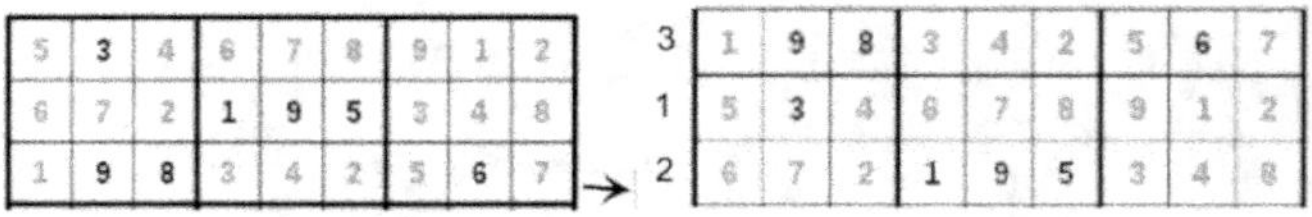

Figure 120: The game will not be ruined by switching between lines, but the music will change in a logical way according to the number distributions.

In this case, instead of the first matrix being 5, 6, 1, it will be 1, 5, 6 where the pitch $C^2_{+59cents}$ represents:

Figure 121: Alternative matrix reading for *Sudoku*.

Sudoku resembles the Bohlen-Pierce in that both are based on a scale that descends from logic. The do, however, have different tone systems. The Bohlen-Pierce scale is a non-octave scale compared to the *Sudoku* scale, which is an octave scale.

8.3 *Sparkling Stone* for solo five- string cello

This is a composition for solo cello that illustrates many spectral microtonal music techniques. The main idea of the composition was that each tone has a logical spectral microtonal connection with the previous tone as is seen in Figure 122. Tone number three in the mentioned figure is *A*, which is the seventh overtone in *G*, the second tone in the figure. Tone *A* represents a branch harmonic series for the *G* main harmonic series forms a main harmonic series for the next tone branch harmonic series *D♯*, the eleventh overtone. The *D♯* branch harmonic series for *A* main fundamental is in its turn a main harmonic series for the next tone, and so on.

Tone number 12, *F#*, is connected to the previous tone *A♯* by a missing fundamental *H* in which *A♯* is the seventh overtone in which *F#* is the third overtone. This relationship between *A♯* and *F#* makes it weaker than the other successive tones which have direct relationship.

Figure 122: *Sparkling Stone* for solo five string cello, C, G, D, A, E.
The melody modulation movement in a microtonal overtone scale.

Another type of indirect relationship can be found between the chords. In Figure 123, all the chords are based on the C main harmonic series, where C is the tone of the first string of the five-string cello.
If the open five strings C, G, D, A, E of the cello are tuned in correspondence to the lowest string C^2, then the following is true:

- G represents the third overtone G_{+2cnts} of the fundamental tone of the main harmonic series C.
- D represents D_{+4cnts}, the third overtone of G_{+2cnts} branch harmonic series and the ninth overtone of the main harmonic series C.
- A represents A_{+6cnts}, the third overtone of D_{+4cnts}, the ninth overtone of the branch harmonic series G_{+4cnts}, and the twenty-seventh overtone of the main harmonic series C.
- E represents E_{+8cnts}, the third overtone of A_{+6cnts}, the ninth overtone of the branch harmonic series D_{+4cnts}, the twenty-seventh overtone of the branch

harmonic series G_{+2cnts}, and the eighty-first overtone of the main harmonic series C.[196]

Figure 123: *Sparkling Stone* for solo five- string cello.
The chordal movement in the C main harmonic series.

From Figure 123, the following relationships are observed:

1- The first basic tones of each chord of the three chords $B♭$, $E♮$ and G are related to the main harmonic series C as seventh, fifth and third overtones.
2- The tones in each chord are connected to the main tone C and they create overtones in its harmonic series.
3- Any harmonic tones or harmonic chords played on these five strings of the cello exist in the main harmonic series of C.

8.4 *Barada* for chamber ensemble

Barada is the river that flows into the quarters of Damascus, the oldest inhabited city in the world. It is one of the chief features in the city. In this piece, I use spectral music to serve the aesthetic musical idea of reflecting my thought towards the Barada River. For example, in the part shown in Figure 124, all instruments play random pitches that belong to a missed fundamental tone C^1. The expected effect is to give the music a mysterious atmosphere, so that a sense of congruence can be felt, but the spectrum timbre changes every second. What results is the same spectrum C^1, but its overtones and timbre vary and change by the change of the pitches and dynamics that the instruments perform at each moment. This part of the piece presents an improvisation in the C^1 spectrum's overtones pitches which I call a blended spectrum.

---

[196] The equation between the main harmonic series and the branch harmonic series is $O_v = O_n * O_b$.
O_v is the overtone number in the main series;
O_n is the overtone number of the branch fundamental in the main series,
and O_b is the number of the overtone in the branch series, or overtone of the overtone.

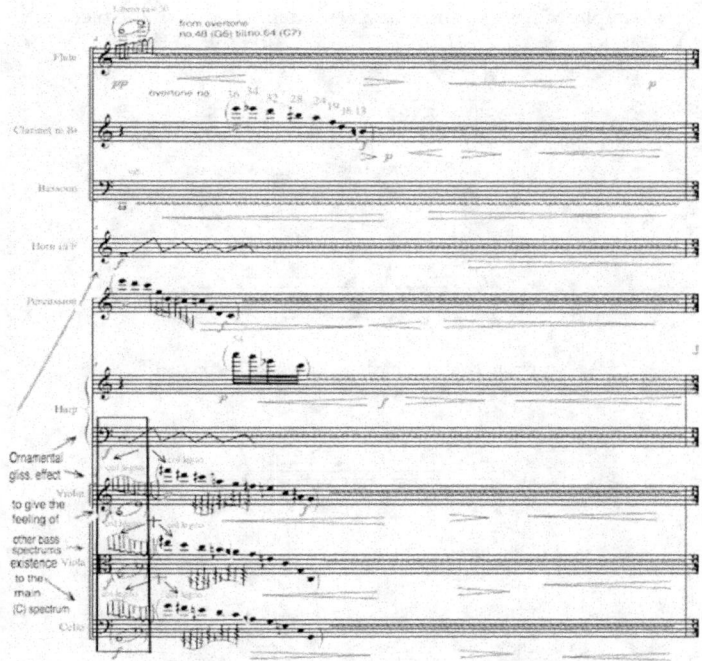

Figure 124: *Barada,* for nine instruments in a blended spectrum. Bar 4 is written in C.M.O.S. to be performed randomly.

In another part of the piece, I try to make a melody based on the *maqam* spectral idea. Many *maqamat* converge as the melody switches between selected notes from the *ajnas* of *maqam* before it moves to a new *maqam*, breaking with the classical *maqamat* modulation, which normally has no more than a third between intervals. I tried to keep other properties of the *maqam*, such as maintain the small intervals while modulating.

Figure 125: *Barada, maqam* modulations.

The main simplified rows of the *maqamat* used in this part of the piece are:

Figure 126: Simplified row of *maqam Mahur* on C.

Figure 127: Simplified row of *maqam Rast* on C.

Figure 128: Simplified row of *maqam Sikah* on E♭.

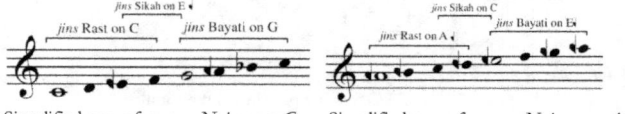

Simplified row of *maqam Nairuz* on C.   Simplified row of *maqam Nairuz* on A♭.

Figure 129: Simplified row of *maqam Nairuz*.

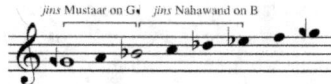

Figure 130: Simplified row of *maqam Mustaar* on G♭.

Most of the previous *maqamat* are based on C, excepting the last *maqam: maqam Musaar* on G♭. All of the tones in the previous *maqamat* exist in the C spectrum, which means that the overtones of the C spectrum can be used in constructing the harmony or other contrapuntal movement in the other tonal levels as accompaniments.

8.5 *Mesopotamian Tears* for woodwinds

In *Mesopotamian Tears* I use a polyphonic harmony for *maqam Husaini*:

Figure 131: Row of *maqam Husaini* on *D*.

In this composition for full orchestra, I use the *ajnas* of the *maqam* in a way I call microtonal polyphony of the *maqam*. In respect to the properties of the *maqam* system, within the context illustrated above, there is an example of western polyphony using the *Husaini* as a source of inspiration and as a way to interpret the content of the theme in *Mesopotamian Tears*. In this part there is a clear polyphonic movement between the three demonstrated instruments. This movement is more Western than Arabic in style. The harmonic structure and the orchestration are very important, as they enrich the Arabic melody, especially when each instrument takes place in performing the melody and the harmony. The dominating mode of *maqam Husaini* will be clearer in this polyphonic style.

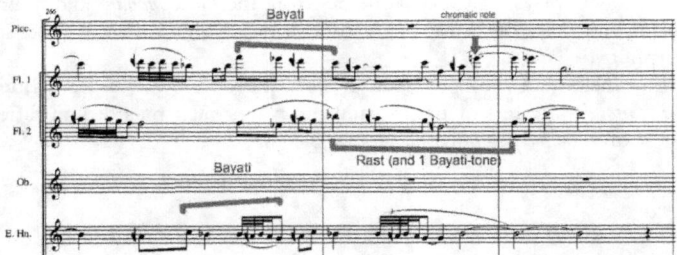

Figure 132: *Mesopotamian tears:* polyphonic movement for melodies written in two *ajnas, jins Bayati* on *C* and *jins Rast* on *D♮*.

In this case, the rules of writing harmony do not directly follow the overtone harmony rules, but instead follow the classical *maqam* mode as there are sometimes multiple C.M.O.S.s. Otherwise, a very high overtone in its C.M.O.S. would be used to write the overtone harmony for the melody. For example, I use polyphony on *maqam Husaini* in a different part of *Qadmoos*, Scene *Antara*:

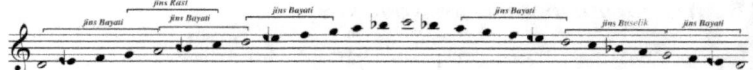

Figure 133: Row of *maqam Husaini* on D.

The overtone which holds this classical *maqam* is the D overtone series, but is higher than the C.M.O.S. overtones which are included in the following illustration:

Figure 134: Overtones from the D overtone series are chosen to the nearest tones in *maqam Husaini* putting into consideration the overtones are written in the 72-TET and the *maqam* is written in the 24-TET.

I took the general random polyphonic music heard when traditional Arabic musicians improvise and play randomly in a melody written in a certain *maqam*, in addition to the ostinato. [197] Normally, Arabic music is written in melodic way, neither harmonic nor polyphonic. When many musicians improvise randomly together on a certain *maqam*, there will be a kind of *maqam*-harmony: each instrument plays a different tone but from the same *maqam*, and when the musicians improvise the same melody but asynchronously there will be a kind of polyphony.

The main melody in the figure below, from the opera *Qadmoos*, is written in *maqam Husaini*. The rest of the instruments play similar melodies in different timing, forming a *maqam* polyphonic mood:

---

[197] For example, El Ghazali, Nazem,
https://www.youtube.com/watch?v=N7FXENPBTzQ..10.2008), Accessed 7 Feb. 2016.

Figure 135: From *Qadmoos*, Storyteller scene (*Anrara, The storyteller starts his game*), Bars 33-36. Polyphonic movement of *maqam Husaini* on D.

In another section of *Mesopotamian Tears,* the numbers in Figure 136 refer to the overtone number, presented by a 24-tone system. This part of the piece is built on the spectrum of a fundamental-tone of C^1. The melodic line and harmonics are built on the same spectrum C^1. The harmony is performed in the third and the fourth octaves of the C^1 spectrum by all strings:

Figure 136: *Mesopotamian Tears,* Bars 326-328: *C* Spectrum in harmony and melody.

8.6 Computer music for random microtonal overtone scales

These pieces were written using the Max/MSP program. The concept was to perform a melody by using the pitches of the M.O.S. The basic elements of the M.O.S. theory are used in this software. The loudness and the duration of the pitches are also considered, for example, if the movement of a pitch is from a low overtone to a higher overtone then the volume will be lower, and if the movement of a pitch is from a high overtone to a lower overtone then the volume will be higher.

Here is a simplified description and illustration of the software: the music begins as soon as the start button is pressed. The start button gives an order to choose a fundamental tone X2 in Hertz, which can be given before, or the computer can choose it according to the given data. In order to start giving non- rhythmical impulses, the time that separates every two impulses is between 500 millisecond (ms) and 2000ms. Next, each impulse generates an overtone number X1 between 8 and 16 in overtone *maqam* or M.O.S. which represents the eight tones of the microtonal overtone scales. The overtone frequency X2 is multiplied by the overtone number X1. For example:

If the fundamental tone frequency (X2) is C1=32.703Hz, and an overtone number (X1) is 5, the audio output frequency will be:

X2*X1= 32.703*5=163,515Hz which is E3$_{-14cents}$

This piece performs a random melody within an octave of a certain scale. It can be demonstrated as follows:

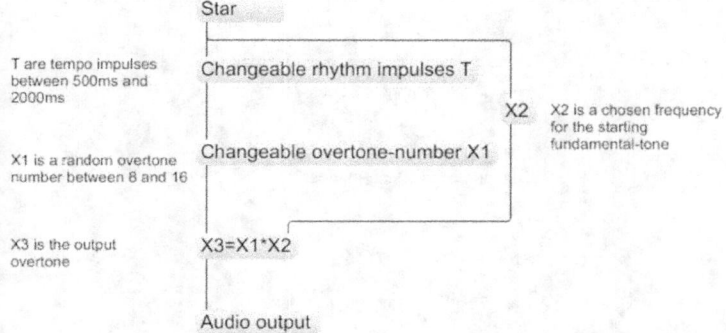

Figure 137: Program performs randomly a melody in a certain M.O.S.

To perform the above melody in different octaves keeping the same microtonal overtone scale, the random number should be multiplied by N=1, 2, 3, etc. depending on the estimated octave. Number 2 means to perform the melody an octave higher, number 3 means to perform the melody in two octaves higher.

N can be also written randomly or according to given data:

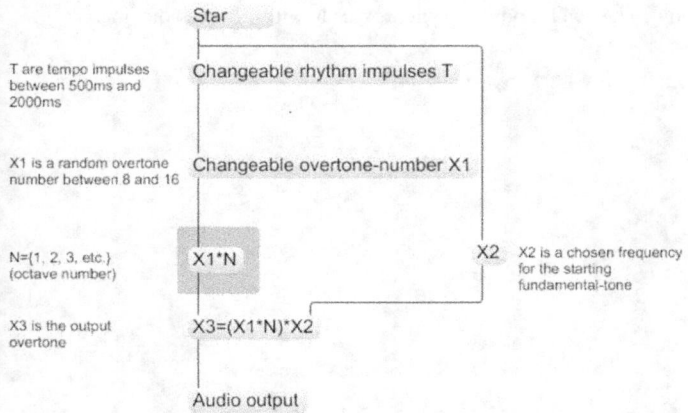

Figure 138: Program performs randomly a melody in a certain M.O.S. in different octaves.

To modulate the melody from a certain microtonal overtone scale to another, the fundamental tone should be changed, which is in the figure (X2). The modulation method is written in the main branch modulation form:

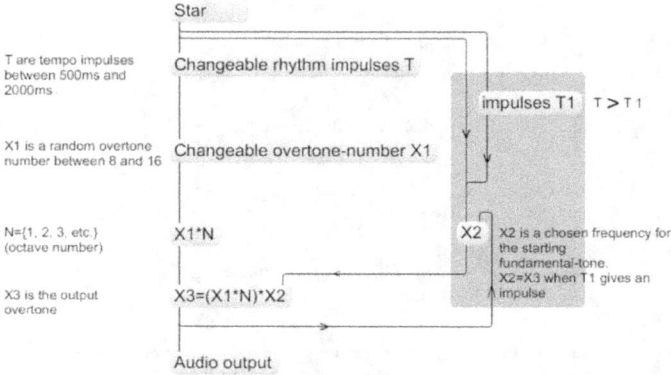

Figure 139: Program performs randomly a melody in M.O.S. This melody modulates from one M.O.S. to another in different octaves.

A simple harmonic method can be applied to the melody of the previous modulated microtonal overtone scales by adding one or more harmonic pitches, each of which is also performed in the same microtonal overtone scale of the melody. They will modulate synchronically with the melodic line.

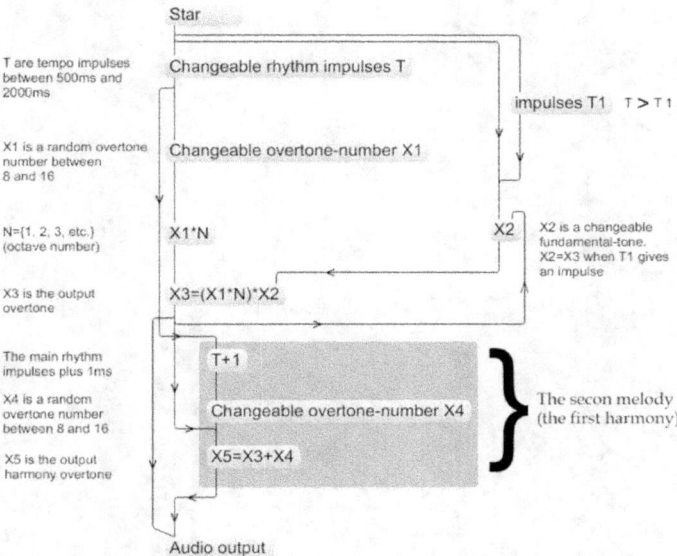

Figure 140: Program randomly performs a melody in M.O.S. accompanied by a parallel harmonic line in M.O.S. This harmony combination modulates from one M.O.S. to another in different octaves

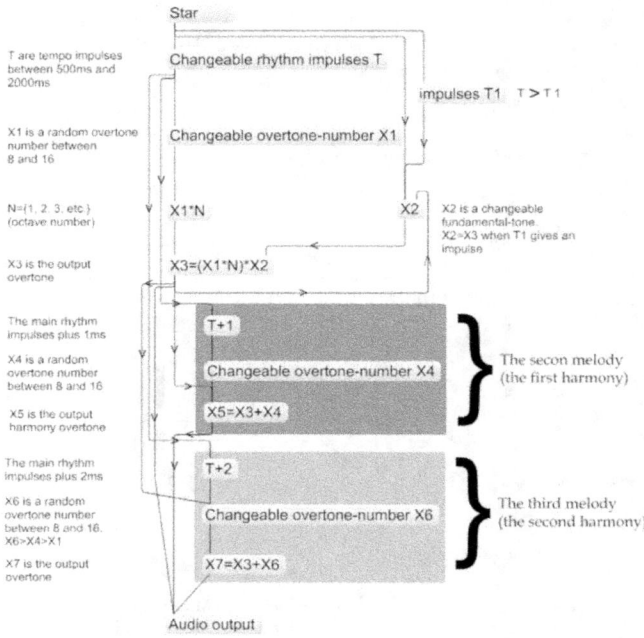

Figure 141: Program randomly performs a melody in M.O.S. accompanied by two parallel harmonic lines in M.O.S. This harmonic combination modulates from one M.O.S. to another in different octaves.

The harmonic overtones of the software can be used in a polyphonic way by separating the tempo impulse T in each voice; in this case, each horizontal voice will be treated as a polyphonic line.

8.7 Opera *Qadmoos*

Qadmoos is the opera using both Arabic and European instruments.

The subject of *Qadmoos* is the unity of humans. It represents hope of further cooperation between the Eastern and Western worlds.

Qadmoos and his brother Europa are the children of Agenor, the king of Tyre. The character Qadmoos is the symbol of the exchange of knowledge between East and West. He took the alphabet to the West while searching for his kidnapped sister. The opera, by bringing life to this legend, shows an old and deep relationship between the European Mediterranean countries.

The libretto of *Qadmoos* was inspired by the myth. After merging the myth into a contemporary context, it works in microtonal spectral cross-cultural music in many aspects:

- The original myth and the libretto have a relationship with the two worlds - A combination of Arabic and Western instruments are used.
- The libretto tells a story which takes place between the two worlds; this is the reason for merging and switching of the musical elements of two different cultures.

8.7.1 Overture analysis

The intervals of the Overture of *Qadmoos* are written mainly in microtonal 72-TET for the spectral music parts. Although this part of the piece is written in a non-melodic way, *maqamat* motives which evoke the *maqam* feeling for a short period are present.

The Overture starts with the fundamental tone D1, performed by the double basses. In bar 18, Figure 142, the violins play high harmonic glissandi to create a feeling of a changeable spectrum with only very high overtones. In bar 19 the gap between the overtones is smaller because other instruments enter playing some missed overtones of the bar before. This gives a new feeling to the same spectrum, and a more concrete feeling at the end of bars 20 and 21.

Figure 142: Strings part of the Overture of *Qadmoos*, Bars. 18-21 demonstrating harmony and melody by using the *D* spectrum. The numbers in the illustration refer to the overtone number.

In a similar harmonic way the woodwind part was written to complete the strings' job:

Figure 142 b: Woodwind part of the Overture of *Qadmoos,* Bars. 20-26 demonstrating harmony and melody. The numbers in the illustration refer to the overtone number.

8.7.2 *Antara*

In this part of the opera I have used different kinds of modulation techniques and tuning systems. To demonstrate the differences among the varieties, some parts of the work have been chosen to be analysed, as they make suitable and variable examples that clarify the basics of the theory.

Multiple Tuning Systems

It is possible to use more than one tuning system to serve the musical idea. Switching between different tuning systems enriches the music with varieties of modes.

Figure 144 is written on *A* microtonal overtone *maqam*. In addition, there are pitches descending from its chromatic microtonal overtone scale Figure 145. The seventeenth overtone *Ais* and the ninteenth overtone *C* of the *A* chromatic microtonal overtone (*A* is number 2 and *C* is number 5 in Figure 145) enrich the harmony, like in the strings section, and the melody, like the tenor section. Compared with the chromatic pitches which are used less often, the pitches of the *A* microtonal overtone scale dominate this part of the piece in the melody and in the harmony. These main pitches of the scale give the *A* microtonal overtone *maqam* its character and mode.

Figure 143: *Qadmoos*, Storyteller Scene (*Antara, The holy war*), Bars.15-16. Overtone-*maqam* on A [A C.M.O.S.]. The red squares illustrate the chromatic overtones.

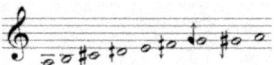

Figure 144: A M.O.S.

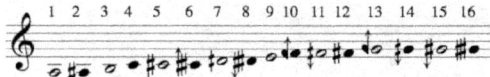

Figure 145: A C.M.O.S.

The next two examples from *Qadmoos* illustrate two kinds of modulation. The first example is for the modulation from one C.M.O.S. to another:

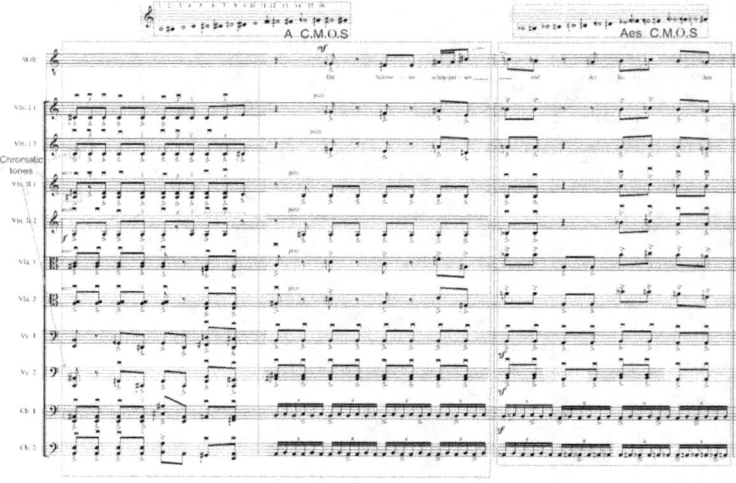

Figure 146: Opera *Qadmoos*, Storyteller Scene (*Antara, The holy war*), Bars 15-16. Modulations between two C.M.O.S.: *A* and *Aes*.

The second example is for the modulation from different tuning systems: from one C.M.O.S. to another. In the example below the modulations are from C.M.O.S. to chromatic 12-TET, and from the last tuning system to *maqamat* system:

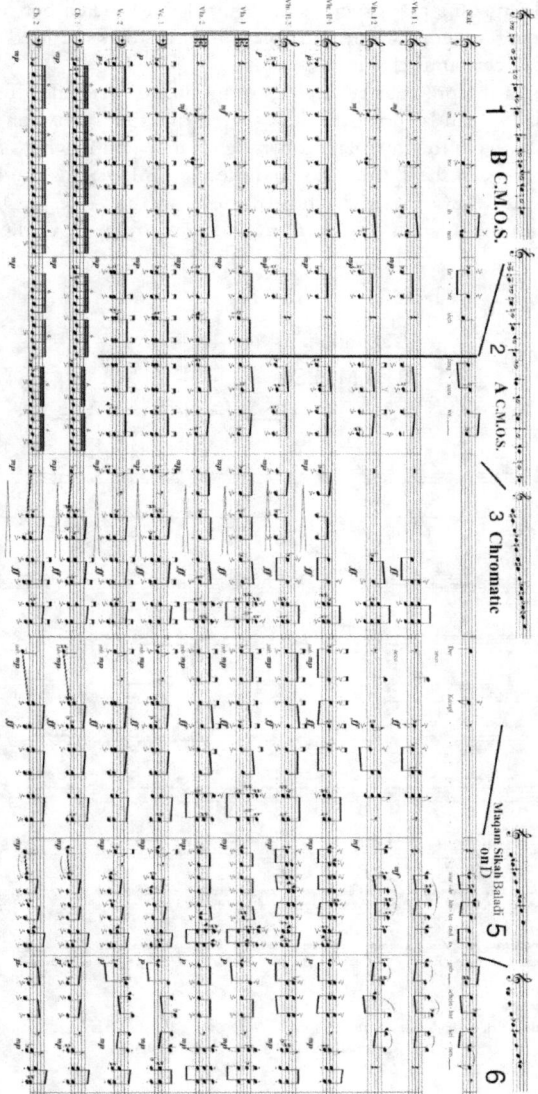

Figure 147: Storyteller Scene (*Antara, The holy war*), Bars 19-24. Modulation between different tuning systems: C.M.O.S., Chromatic scale and *maqam*.

It is possible in some cases such as in Figure 147 to switch between different kinds of tuning systems, where multiple tuning systems are used to serve the process of a special musical idea.

The process in the previous example is to modulate between different modes. This modulation can be done through shared overtones between two successive C.M.O.S.s as in the modulation between Bars 1 and 2, where B is a modulating tone between the B C.M.O.S. and the $A\flat$ C.M.O.S., as the fundamental tone in this B C.M.O.S. is the ninth overtone in the $A\flat$ C.M.O.S. This is a branch main modulation (/−|); a modulation from B C.M.O.S. to $A\flat$ C.M.O.S:

Figure 148: Storyteller Scene (*Antara, The holy war*), Bar .29-31. Modulation (/−|) from B C.M.O.S. to $A\flat$ C.M.O.S.

Although there are two different tuning systems between any shared tones as in *A♭, A, B, H, E♭, F*, these shared tones have similar intervals from to the fundamental tone as is illustrated below:

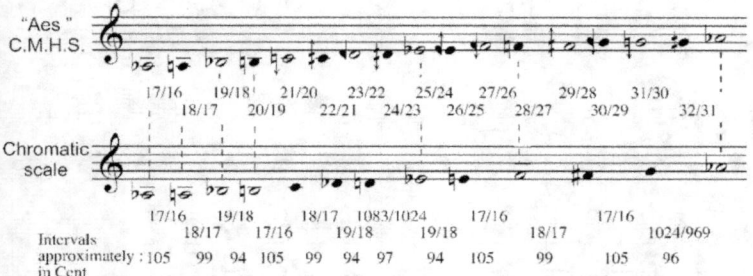

Figure 149: Chromatic 12-tone scale derived from the C.M.O.S.

The third kind of modulation in this part of the composition is the modulation to a new *maqam*. This *maqam* has no clear traditional existence; it has a new category for its *ajnas* and is not an overtone *maqam*.

The fifth bar is written in the following *maqam* scale considering the shared tones with the previous chromatic scale *D, G, C#*:

Figure 150: Overtonal simplified row of *maqam* with new category for the *ajnas*.

The bar marked with number six in Figure 151 is written in a *maqam* that has *jins-Sikah* as a main *jins* giving the mode the *Sikah* character, although it has a different category from *maqam Sikah*.[198] This main *jins Sikah* is also in the mode of the previous *maqam*; this *jins* dominates both measures although it functions in the second measure as a transposition to the first one:

Figure 152: A simplified row of overtonal *maqam* with new category for the *ajnas*.

---

[198] See the row *maqam Sikah,* Figure 98.

Figure 153: Storyteller Scene (*Antara, The holy war*), Bars 22-24. Modulation for the chromatic overtonal *maqamat* from C to D and then from D to H♮.

In addition to the previous modules of modulations, it is also possible for a random modulation to go from a certain M.O.S. to another without any preparation for the modulation.

It is also possible to modulate while keeping the previous M.O.S. In this case there will be two M.O.S.s: the sub-harmonic and the new main M.O.S. (see Figure 153). The vocal line remains in the previous main M.O.S. of the instruments of the previous bar, while the instruments play in the third branch M.O.S. of the vocal line in the same measure:

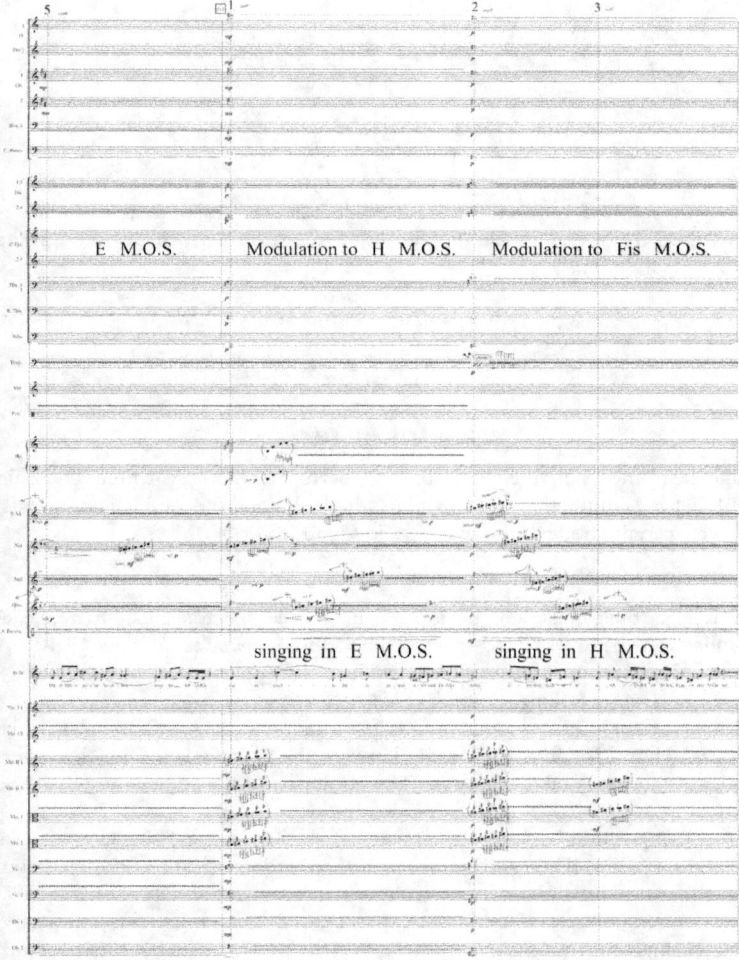

Figure 154: *Antara* scene: Modulation to the third M.O.S.:E M.O.S. modulates to H M.O.S. and then to Fis M.O.S. The vocal part keeps on singing the fundamental for the third B.O.S. which other instruments perform.

In Figure 154 the orchestral instruments perform in E M.O.S. mode, however randomly:

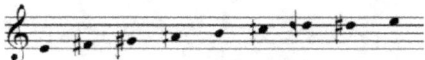

Figure 155: E M.O.S.

Thus, this mode dominates the music while it is performed, then it modulates to its third, H M.O.S., while the vocal line keeps on performing in the same M.O.S. (E M.O.S.):

Figure 156: H M.O.S.

Some instruments in the orchestra can perform randomly within a certain M.O.S., for example the second violins, the violas and the Arabic instruments, to give a certain mode to the music, as in Figure 154.

Imitating the alphabet pronunciation

In my electronic music compositions I have used spectral music to replicate sounds from nature such as in my composition *Schwimmende Vögel* (2010). A Synthi AKS synthesizer was used to produce electronic sounds imitating birds, wind, sea waves, strolling on sand, etc.

Another example of imitating sounds from nature is in the Storyteller Scene *(Antara)*: Here I found a relationship between the pronunciation for the different letters and musical instruments. The vocal part of the composition is in the German.

In this composition I try to differentiate between the letters, by giving each its spectral character. This method needs a good understanding of the spectrum of each musical instrument in the orchestra.

Here are some examples for some experiments I have done with letters, and other examples for musical instruments which are used to serve the main idea of the spectral composition. I shall not go in an in-depth analysis of the phonetics and their spectrums, as it is not a priority for my theory.

In the traditional Western the alphabet is divided into two main groups: vowels and consonants.[199] Most vocal melodic writing in western music emphasizes the vowels as constant tones. The consonants normally share the same tone

---

[199] Jones, Daniel. *An outline of English Phonetics*. Cambridge UP, Cambridge 1976, p.xvii.

of the vowels. For example, the notation of a word like "Strong" will be focused on O, as the word only has one syllable. This composed melody for this word can be written in one tone or more.

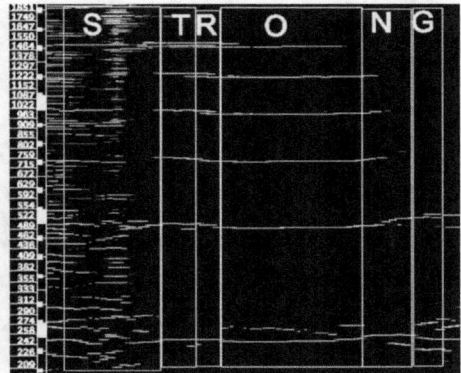

Figure 157: Spectrogram analysis for a female voice saying "Strong" with an American accent, stressing the S and keeping the duration of O for longer than the other letters.

The reason behind this treatment for the tones is that the vowels have clear overtones. In addition to that, using vowels makes it easy to move between tones. It is however difficult to change the tones or to give clear tones by using the consonants and it can be difficult to hold the tone for long time for other letters.[200]

In the previous example the letter S is more enharmonic than the other letters, but it can last for some time. O is the most harmonic letter it lasts longer. N and G have more amplitude for the overtones of the lower frequency overtones than the upper frequency overtones, contrary to the T and R. G, which can be categorized as a velar plosive, cannot last for very long. The amplitude of the lower frequency overtones is still higher than the amplitude of the lower frequency overtones of the letters S, T, R, O, and N (see Figure 156).[201]

Letters are classified in different groups. The main classifications for the consonants are plosive, nasal, trill, tap or flap, fricative, lateral fricative, approximant, and lateral approximant.

---

[200] Ladefoged, Peter & Keith Johnson. *A Course in Phonetics*. Cengage Learning, Stamford 2006, p.60.
[201] Ladefoged, Peter & Sandra Ferrari Disner. *Vowels and Consonants*. 3rd ed. Harcourt Brace Jovanovich, 2012, pp.68–85.

These groups are divided into sub-groups: bilabial, labiodental, dental, alveolar, post alveolar, retroflex, palatal, velar, uvular, pharyngeal, and glottal.[202]
Figures 157 and 158 illustrate the change of the spectrum for the same male sound while pronouncing S and the Sh. The concentration of the high amplitude overtones of S are located in the higher frequencies and in Sh they are located in a lower frequency.

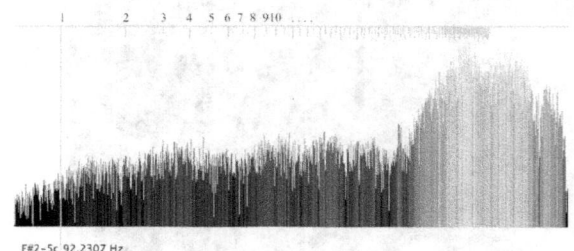

Figure 158: A male sound has a normal frequency of 90. 2307 Hz when pronouncing the letter S.

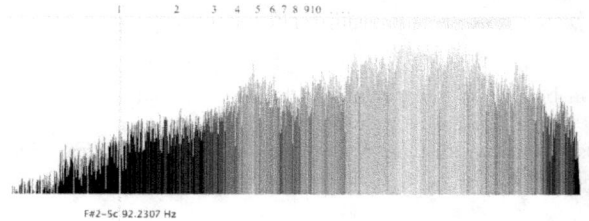

Figure 159: A male sound has a normal frequency of 90. 2307 Hz when pronouncing Sh.

---

[202] Ashby, Patricia. *Speech Sounds*. Routledge, London 2008, p.66.

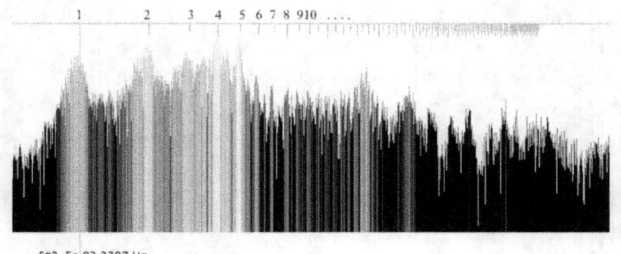

Figure 160: A male sound has a normal frequency of 90.2307 Hz when pronouncing *Ga*.

In the Storyteller scene in *Qadmoos*, I tried to imitate the pronunciation of each letter of the sung words by using a talking orchestra.

For example, in Figure 161, the orchestra plays the letter S by using the timbre of the cymbal accompanied by piccolo, harmonic tones in the violins and a quiet fundamental tone of an oboe. The cymbal and the harmonic tones of the violins give the noise effect feeling of the letter S especially in the range of high frequencies. In addition, the quiet piccolo and the fundamental tone in the oboe give the sound its timbre, stability and shape. [203]

The hissing sounds S and the Sh are both to be more enharmonic. To imitate the Sh sound as performed by the orchestra to resemble the tenor, the noise is concentrated on the alto instruments rather than the soprano. The enharmonic overtones of the percussion instruments and the noise effects on other instruments can perform these two letters by using special techniques like the movement of a guitar pick along the metal strings of the harp or the qanoon.

When starting to pronounce the letters G, B, D, T, the tongue position cannot last very long, and the sound goes directly to a vowel sound (see Figure 158). The beginnings of these letters are presented in different ways and in different techniques, such as staccato and pizzicato in Gung, Big-Drum, Timpani, Strings in low registers, etc. These instruments are mainly used to give the expression for the starting of the letter.

---

[203] Olive, Joseph P., Alice Greenwood, & John Coleman. *Acoustics of American English Speech.* Springer-Verlag, New York 1993, pp.92–95.

Figure 161: Storyteller Scene (*Antara, The gang leader's will*), Bars 1–6. Spectral microtone orchestration is written as an imitation to the letters of the vocal part. It is written mainly in F M.O.S.

It is important to know how to imitate the movement of the overtones when the singer moves from one letter to another inside a word, and how the singer stops or starts to pronounce a word by using the acoustic properties of the consonants. [204] These properties can be simulated by the acoustics of orchestral instruments, and also by using suitable technique in the instrument, such as pizzicato, or staccato.

Additionally, the first violins are divided into three groups, the first two of which are dedicated to giving the feeling of the high overtones.

---

[204] Gut, Ulrike. *Introduction to English Language Phonetics and Phonology*. Textbooks in English Language and Phonology. Magnus Huber & Joybrato Mukherjee, eds., Peter Lang, Frankfurt 2009, p.156–157.

9 Conclusion

Towards a Spectral Microtonal Composing: A Bridge between Arabic and Western Music explains a new musical theory. It presents a new concept that connects traditional Arabic music to contemporary music and brings Arabic music to spectral music and overtone music.

To prove the theory and demonstrate its main goal, many compositions have been included to underline the main elements of the theory: traditional Arabic music tuning system (*maqam*), microtonal music, and spectral music.

It is important to establish a clear definition and to determine the reasons for using the basic elements of the theory, mainly for the *maqam*, which are found in two different concepts of tuning systems. The first concept is the mathematical one, based on theories written between the eighth and fourteenth centuries. The last theoretical development for this tuning system was at the beginning of the twentieth century where the intervals of the *maqamat* were fixed in one tuning system (24-TET). The second concept is the practical fact for the *maqamat* in which its intervals are inherited and developed from one generation to another and from one region to another. These two concepts give the *maqam* its varieties and flexibility.

This flexibility of the *maqam* allowed me to divide the theory into two kinds of overtone *maqamat*. The first overtone *maqam* can be found within the first 16 overtones within the harmonic series M.O.S., or it can be derived from the first 32 overtones in the harmonic series C.M.O.S. It is created without adding extra overtones to those of the same harmonic series.

The second *maqam* is more traditional. It is created by adding *ajnas* from different overtone series and letting the main overtone series perform a few overtones.

To have the feeling of the traditional Arabic music tuning system in both types of overtone *maqamat* and in spectral contemporary music, it is necessary to take into consideration the properties and the character of the *maqam*.

It is also important to give basic descriptions of the relationship between the overtones in harmonic overtones and the harmonic relationship between two or more tones playing certain overtones in harmonic series.

This research has led to the conclusion that *maqam* music can be used in microtonal spectral music, within the M.O.S and the C.M.O.S; however, the properties of the *maqam* should be maintained.

To establish proof of the previous concept in this theory, it was important to write some compositions including mathematics in music such as in the piece *Sudoku*, which has new procedures to connect between mathematical concepts and microtonal music.

In addition to using the Sudoku game, microtonal harmony, *maqam* and spectral music are used in sound experiments in other compositions including *Secrets, Barada, Eunus, Flowers Ceremony of Sadness, Sparkling a Stone,* and *Amira and the Elephant.*

The opera *Qadmoos* carries the main elements of the theoretical concept, and was composed the theories explored in Chapter 5 and 6 of this book. It is a composition for full orchestra with a smaller group of Arabic instruments similar to a concerto grosso. All conceptual traits of the main theory are prominent in this composition

My study of computer and electronic music at the *Hochschule für Musik und Theater Hamburg* for two years has been of great help to learn more about sound design and to run experiments which are difficult to do with acoustic instruments, mainly that it is much easier to have precise microtones and overtones by using computer and electronic music.

Additionally, personal analysis for tuning-systems in Arabic music and in other types of music in the world has been done to compare between the theoretical hypotheses of these tuning-systems of these cultures with the actual traditional music. This research was run while I was teaching at Carl von Ossietzky University of Oldenburg.

10 Perspective of the theory

This study can open new research possibilities to build bridges between different traditional musics and the spectral and overtonal microtone music through new concepts in melody and harmony.

It motivates researchers who are looking for ways to design new musical instruments and new tuning systems. In addition, it facilitates the work of composers who are looking for a way to connect different cultures in their work.

Bibliography

Adler, Samuel. *The Study of Orchestration*. W. W. Norton & Company Inc., New York 2002.

Al-Humssi, Umar Abd-Al-Rahman. *Usool Aliqaat Alsharqieh ua Diraseh Tahlilieh fi al-Maqamat Alarabieh/ The Origin of the Oriental Rhythms and an Analysis Study in the Arabic Maqamat*. Al-Assad Library-Press, Damascus 1992.

Ashby, Patricia. *Speech Sounds*. Routledge, New York 2008.

Ashton, Anthony. *Harmonograph*. Wooden Books, Wales 2003.

Atkinson, Charles M. *The Critical Nexus Tone-System, Mode, and Notation in Early Medieval Music*. Oxford University Press, New York 2009.

Bartolozzi, Bruno. *New Sounds for Woodwind*. Oxford University Press, London 1967.

Benson, David J. *Music: A Mathematical Offering*. Cambridge University Press, Cambridge 2008.

Burt, Peter. *The Music of Toru Takemitsu*. Cambridge University Press, Cambridge 2003.

Busoni, Ferruccio. *Entwurf einer neuen Ästhetik der Tonkunst*. Insel, Frankfurt am Main 1974.

Clark, Xenos. *The American Naturalist, Animal Music, its Nature and Origin*, vol.xiii. The University of Chicago Press, Chicago 1879.

Cope, David. *Virtual Music*. MIT Press, Cambridge 2004.

Cornicello, Anthony. *Timbral Organization in Tristan Murail's "Désintégrations" and "Rituals"*. PhD thesis. Brandeis University, Massachusetts 2000.

Crickmore, Leon. *New Light on the Babylonian Tonal System. Proceedings of the International Conference of Near Easten Archaeomusicology: held at the British Museum, December 4, 5 and 6, 2008*, ICONEA, London 2010.

Daniélou, Alain. *Music and The Power of Sound*. Inner Traditions, Rochester 1995.

Dufourt, Hugues. *Musique spectrale*. Société Nationale de Radiodiffusion, Radio-France, March 1979. Reprinted in *Conséquences* nos 7–8, Paris 1986.

El-Mahdi, Salah. *La Musique Arabe*. Alphonse Leduc, Paris 1972.

Farhat, Hormoz. *The Dastgah Concept in Persian Music*. Cambridge University Press, Cambridge 2004.

Fineberg, Joshua. *Classical Music, Why Bother?* Routledge, New York 2006.

Gut, Ulrike. *Introduction to English Language Phonetics and Phonology*. Magnus Huber & Joybrato Mukherjee, eds. Textbooks in English Language and Phonology, Peter Lang, Frankfurt 2009.

Haba, Alois. *New Theory of Harmony, of the Diatonic, the Chromic, the Quarter-tone, the Third-tone, the Sixth-tone, and the Twelfth-tone System*. Universal Education A. G., Wien 1978.

Heinz-Klaus, Metzger & Riehn, Rainer. *Musik-Konzepte Sonderband Musik der anderen Tradition. Mikrotonale Tonwelten*. Richard Borrberg, München 2003.

Husmann, Heinrich. *Grundlagen Derantiken und Orientalischen Musikkultur*. Walter de Gruyter & Co., Berlin 1961.

Jones, Daniel. *An outline of English Phonetics*. Cambridge University Press, Cambridge 1976.

Karkoschka, Erhard. *Notation in New Music*. Universal Education, London 1972.

Kartomi, Margaret & et al. "*Indonesia*." In *The Garland Handbook of Southeast Asian Music*. Terry E. Miller & Sean Williams, ed. Routledge, Abingdon 2008.

Keller, Kjell. *Klaus Huber und die arabische Musik, Begegnungen, Entgrenzungen, Berührungen*. Dissonanz, no. 88, December, Basel 2004.

Ladefoged, Peter & Johnson, Keith. *A Course in Phonetics*. Cengage Learning, Stamford 2006.

Ladefoged, Peter & Disner, Sandra Ferrari. *Vowels and Consonants*. 3rd ed., Wiley-Blackwell, Chichester 2012.

Lahiri, Aditi. *The Grammar of Carnatic Music*. Walter de Gruyter GmbH & Co. KG, Berlin 2007.

Ligeti, György Sándo. *Lontano*. Schott, Mainz 1967.

Loy, Gareth R. *Musimathics, The Mathematical Foundations of Music*. vol.1, MIT Press, Cambridge 2006.

Maalouf, Shireen. *History of Arabic Music Theory*. Kaslik, Lebanon 2002.

Manik, Liberty. *Das Arabische Tonsystem im Mittelalter*. E. J. Brill, Leiden 1969.

McAdams, Stephen & Daniel Matzkin. *The Roots of Musical Variation in Perceptual Similarity and Invariance*. In *The Cognitive Neuroscience of Music*. Isabelle Peretz & Robert J. Zatorre, eds., Oxford University Press, Oxford 2003.

McClain, Ernest G. *The Pythagorean Plato*. Nicolas-Hays, Inc., York beach 1984.

McClain, Ernest G. *The Myth Of Invariance*. Nicolas-Hays, Inc., York beach 1984.

McClain, Ernest. *A Sumerian Text in Quantified Archaeomusicology*. In *Proceedings of the International Conference of Near Eastern Archaeomusicolog y ICONEA 2008*, Richard Dumbrill & Irving Finkel, eds., Lulu, London 2010.

Metzger, Heinz-Klaus & Rainer Riehn. *Musik-Konzepte Sonderband Musik der anderen Tradition. Mikrotonale Tonwelten*. Richard Borrberg, München 2003.

Miranda, Eduardo Reck. *Computer Sound Design*. Focal Press, Oxford 2002.

Mitchell, Terence. *Another Look at Alleged Ancient Bagpipes*. In *Proceedings of the International Conference of Near Eastern Archaeomusicolog y ICONEA 2008*. Richard Dumbrill & Irving Finkel, eds., Lulu, London 2010.

Myer, Jürgen. *Acoustics and the Performance of Music*. Springer, Braunschweig 2009.

Nidel, Richard. *World Music, The Basics*. Routledge, London 2005.

Nolan, Catherine. *Music theory and mathematics*. In *The Cambridge History of Music. The Cambridge history of Western music theory*. Thomas Christensen, ed. Cambridge UP, Cambridge 2008.

Olive, Joseph P., Alice Greenwood, & John Coleman. *Acoustics of American English Speech*. Springer-Verlag, New York 1993.

Olson, Harry F. *Music, Physics and Engineering*. Dover Publications, New York 1967.

Parker, Barry R. *Good Vibrations*. Johns Hopkins UP, Baltimore 2009.

Pasler, Jann. *Writing Through Music*. Oxford UP, New York 2008.

Partch, Harry. *Genesis of a Music*. Da Capo Press, New York 1974.

Peretz, Isabelle & Robert J. Zatorre, eds. *The Cognitive Neuroscience of Music*. Oxford UP, Oxford 2003.

Persichetti, Vincent. *Twentieth-Century Harmony*. W. W. Norton & Company, New York 1961.

Reinhard Kurt. *Chinesische Musik*. Erich Röth-Verlag, Kassel 1956.

Sadie, Stanley, ed. *The New Grove Dictionary of Music and Musicians*. 2nd ed. vol.24, Macmillan Publishers Limited, London 2001.

Schuler, Thomas Herwig. *Mikrotonalität und ihre Wurzeln bei Harry Partch*. In *Musikzeit. Mikrotonal Komponieren*. Marion Diederichs-Lafite, ed. ÖMZ, Wien 2007–08.

Sethares, William A. *Tuning, Timbre, Spectrum, Scale*. 2nd ed. London 2005.

Stroh, Wolfgang M. *midi-pädagogische schriftenreihe*. Heft 10, 2 Disketten musiklabor, Berlin, Berlin1994.

Touma, Habib Hassan. *The Music of the Arabs*. Amadeus Press, Oxford 2003.

Williams, Andy C.F. *The Aristoxenian Theory of Musical Rhythm*. Cambridge UP, Cambridge 2009.

Web References

Altoft, Stephen. *Microtonal Trumpet*. Official page.
http://www.microtonaltrumpet.com/

Carrillo, Julian. *Julian Carillo y el Sonido 13, Revolucion del Sonido 13*.
http://www.sonido13.com/sonido13.html, 11.07.2009

El Ghazali, Nazem (1921– 1963).
https://www.youtube.com/watch?v=N7FXENPBTzQ

Fakhri, Sabah. *Jadaka L-Ghaith.*
http://www.youtube.com/watch?v=MWyo0R88Oug

Farraj, Johnny. *Maqam World.*
http://maqamworld.com/ajnas.html

Grosskopf, Erhard.
http://www.erhardgrosskopf.de/texte-engl.htm

Hajdu, Georg.
http://georghajdu.de/6-2/macaque/

Helmut, Bayerischer Rundfunk.
http://www.erhardgrosskopf.de/texte-engl.htm

Huun Huur Tu at Philadelphia Folk Festival, August 2006.
(http://www.youtube.com/watch?v=RxK4pQgVvfg

*Huun Huur Tu at Philadelphia Folk Festival, August 2006.*http://www.youtube.com/watch?v=RxK4pQgVvfg&feature=kp

Javanese Gamelan.
https://www.youtube.com/watch?v=Il5nGXComn0

Joly, Gordon. *The Six Senses.*
http://sense-think-act.org/index.php?title=Senses

Keller, Kjell. *Klaus Huber und die arabische Musik, Begegnungen, Entgrenzungen, Berührungen.* Dissonanz, No.. 88, Dec. 2004, pp.14–20.
http://www.dissonance.ch/upload/pdf/088_14_hb_kjk_huber.pdf

Klingbeil, Michael. *SPEAR* software program.
http://www.klingbeil.com/spear/

Krishnaraj, S. *Carnatic India: Carnatic Music History and Evolution*, 2006–15.
http://www.carnaticindia.com/carnatic_music.html

Mabury, Brett. *An investigation into the spectral music idiom and its association with visual imagery, particularly that of film and video.*
http://ro.ecu.edu.au/cgi/viewcontent.cgi?article=1129&context=theses

Mills, Merope. "Composer reinvents the piano." The Guardian. 1 Feb. 2013.
http://www.theguardian.com/uk/2003/feb/01/arts.artsnews1

Parfitt, David. *The Oud*.
http://www.oud.eclipse.co.uk/index.html

Playing the congo / thumbpiano / akogo.
https://www.youtube.com/watch?v=u_7e2sbetkU

Schwarz, Diemo & Matthew Wright. *Extensions and Applications of the SDIF Sound Description Interchange Format*. Proceedings of the International Computer Music Conference. Ircam, 2000.
http://recherche.ircam.fr/anasyn/schwarz/publications/icmc2000/sdif-extensions.pdf

Stroh, Wolfgang M. Official website.
http://www.musik-for.uni-oldenburg.de/planet/index1.html

Walker, Elaine. *The Bohlen-Pierce Scale: Continuing Research*. Final Project in Advanced Acoustics, NYU, 2001.
http://ziaspace.com/NYU/BP-Scale_research.pdf

Waxman, Ken. *Microtonal Brass*.
http://www.onefinalnote.com/uaa/2005/unamerican41/

Tables

Table 1: Way to have the main tones in *Bohlen–Pierce* Scale. 10
Table 2: Ratios of main tones in the *Bohlen–Pierce Scale*. 10
Table 3: Intervals in *Bohlen–Pierce Scale*. 10
Table 4: Diamond and the 43-Ton-scale of H.Partch. 11
Table 5: 22 *srutis* in the *Hindustani* scale. 16
Table 6: First 192 overtones of a tone C1 (32.703 Hz) spectrum. 28
Table 7: Series of the branch overtones comparable to the main overtone series. 41
Table 8: Possible *ajnas* in an overtone scale compared to classical Arabic *ajnas*. 89

Figures

Figure 1: *Ptolemy's Syntonic Diatonic* Scale 8
Figure 2: Scale from the harmonic series in the fourth octave 8
Figure 3: Scale from the harmonic series in the fifth octave 8
Figure 4: Pythagorean diatonic scale 9
Figure 5: Balinese *pélog* (saih 7) Krobokan village 14
Figure 6: *Sléndro* scale from gender dasa, Kuta village 14
Figure 7: Comparing *pélog* scale with *sléndro* scales 15
Figure 8: *Sléndro* scale and *pélog* scale from Bali gamelan examples for *prélog* scale and one for *sléndro* scale 15
Figure 9: Intervals in an *Akogo* 16
Figure 10: Names of the intervals within a major second (from *C* to *D*) in Arabic Music 24
Figure 11: Accidentals used in my composition 25
Figure 12: First 64 overtones converted to musical pitches of a fundamental tone C1 (32.703 Hz) spectrum 29
Figure 13: Hypothetical spectrum paragraph of 16 overtones 32
Figure 14: Observed measurements of tone spectrum developments in time for three C4 staccato tones 33
Figure 15: Sonogram showing the low *D* on a *Nai* played crescendo and then diminuendo 33
Figure 16: First four octaves of the overtone series 35
Figure 17: Illustration for a symbolic tree comparing it with the overtones of the sound 36
Figure 18: Categorizing the pitches of the first four octaves of the overtone series due to their strength and the microtonal overtone scale. 37

Figure 19: Chromatic microtonal overtone scale which is placed in the sixth octave of the C1 overtone series...38
Figure 20: Branch harmonic series of the third overtone in C1 main harmonic series...42
Figure 21: Branch harmonic series of the fifth overtone in C1 main harmonic series...42
Figure 22: Branch harmonic series of the seventh overtone in C1 main harmonic series 42
Figure 23: Branch harmonic series of the ninth overtone in C1 main harmonic series...42
Figure 24: Branch harmonic series of the thirteenth overtone in C1 main harmonic series. 43
Figure 25: Branch harmonic series of the fifteenth overtone in C1 main harmonic series 43
Figure 26: Branch harmonic series of the seventeenth overtone in C1 main harmonic series 43
Figure 27: Shared overtones between two tones are played in unison C1, C1.44
Figure 28: Constructed fundamental tone wave interference from two fundamentals of two tones are played in unison C1, C1............................45
Figure 29: Second possible interval from C1..45
Figure 30: Shared overtone between the main tone C1 and the branch overtone series of the second harmonic accompanying tone C2 45
Figure 31: Constructive fundamental tone wave interference for two fundamentals of two tones the second tone plays the frequency of the second overtone of the first tone; one octave higher C1, C2....................45
Figure 32: Movement toward the undertone...46
Figure 33: Overtone series and undertone series for C4 fundamental 47
Figure 34: Shared overtones between the main tone C2 and the branch overtone series of the accompanying tone C1 47
Figure 35: (I, 3)..48
Figure 36: (I, 3^) tone movement from a main-tone C2 to its sixth branch tone (G4$_{+2cnts}$) in higher octave...49
Figure 37: (I, 3v) tone movement from a main-tone C2 to its third branch-tone G2$_{+2cnts}$ within an octave. 50
Figure 38: (I, 9) tone movement from a main-tone C to its ninth branch-tone D$_{+4cnts}$ within an octave. 50
Figure 39: (I,-5) tone down movement from main tone C to a branch-tone G1$_{+2cnts}$. 51
Figure 40: (3, I) tone movement from a branch-tone G1$_{+2cnts}$ to its main-tone C..52
Figure 41: Comparing the overtones in the G3 harmonic series to the overtones in the C1 harmonic series...52
Figure 42: (3, I) tone movement from a branch overtone G1$_{+2cnts}$ to a lower main-tone C..52

Figure 43: (3, I) tone movement from a branch-tone $G1_{+2cnts}$ to a main tone C within an octave 53
Figure 44: $G1_{+2cnts}$ harmonic series compared to C1 harmonic series.. The fundamental $G1_{+2cnts}$ is not included in the overtones of the main harmonic series of C1. 54
Figure 45: Undertones from $G2_{+2cnts}$ sub-harmonic series 54
Figure 46: (3, I) tone movement to the third overtone within an octave 54
Figure 47: Categorization for the movement of two microtonal harmonics related to the order of overtone numbers of the microtonal overtone scale, starting from the overtones nearer to the fundamental 57
Figure 48: Movement from the unison to the other tones in the microtonal overtone scale. 57
Figure 49: Movement from the second tone in the microtonal overtone scale to the other tones. 58
Figure 50: Movement from the third tone in the microtonal overtone scale to the other tones. 59
Figure 51: Movement from the fourth tone in the microtonal overtone scale to the other tones. 59
Figure 52: The movement from the fifth tone in the microtonal overtone scale to the other tones. 60
Figure 53: Movement from the sixth tone in the microtonal overtone scale to the other tones. 60
Figure 54: Movement from the seventh tone in the microtonal overtone scale to the other tones. 61
Figure 55: Movement from the eighth tone in the microtonal overtone scale to the other tones. 61
Figure 56: Movement from the ninth tone in the microtonal overtone scale to the other tones. 62
Figure 57: The first interval represents the first overtone. The second interval represents the tones of the overtone scale. 62
Figure 58: The first interval represents the second overtone. The second interval represents the tones of the overtone scale. 63
Figure 59: The first interval represents the third overtone. The second interval represents the tones of the overtone scale. 63
Figure 60: The first interval represents the fifth overtone. The second interval represents the tones of the overtone scale. 64
Figure 61: The first interval represents the seventh overtone. The second interval represents the tones of the overtone scale. 64
Figure 62: The first interval represents the ninth overtone. The second interval represents the tones of the overtone scale. 64
Figure 63: The first interval represents the eleventh overtone. The second interval represents the tones of the overtone scale. 65
Figure 64: The first interval represents the thirteenth overtone. The second interval represents the tones of the overtone scale. 65

Figure 65: The first interval represents the fifteenth overtone. The second interval represents the tones of the overtone scale. 65
Figure 67: Similarity in transition. 68
Figure 68: Four tones in harmony from the *C* microtonal overtone scale 69
Figure 69: Five tones in harmony from the *C* microtonal overtone scale 69
Figure 70: Inversions of nine tones from the *C* microtonal overtone scale classified according to the category of their position from the fundamental. 70
Figure 71: Nine tones represent the microtonal overtone scale tones. They are moving to a high stable chord. 71
Figure 72: Nine tones represent the microtonal overtone-scale tones. 71
Figure 73: Cluster for the tones of the *C* microtonal overtone-scale. 72
Figure 74: Modulation from the overtone tuning system of *C* to the overtone tuning system of D_{+4cnts} 73
Figure 75: Overtone harmonic movement from $E_{-14cnts}$ to C_{+0cnt}. 73
Figure 76: Overtone harmony modulation from C_{+0cnt} to $E_{-53cnts}$ through the thirteenth overtone. 74
Figure 77: Random overtone harmony modulation from C_{+0cnt} to A_{+0cnt}. 75
Figure 78: Overtone harmonic modulation from C_{+0cnt} to D_{+4cnts} through the ninth overtone of *C*. 76
Figure 79: Overtone harmonic movement from $E_{-14cnts}$ to C_{+0cnt} through the fundamental and the fifth $E_{-14cnts}$ and the fifteenth $H_{-12cnts}$ overtones 76
Figure 80: Overtone harmonic movement from $E_{-14cnts}$ to C_{+0cnt}. 77
Figure 81: Overtone harmonic movement from C_{+0cnt} to G_{+2cnts} through the fifteenth overtone. 77
Figure 82: *Maqam Ajam* on B-flat written in 24-TET/ major scale on B-flat written in 12-TET. 80
Figure 83: One of al-Urawi heptatonic tuning-system rows written in the 12-TET or in the 24-TET. 80
Figure 84: Al-Urawi heptatonic tuning-system rows written in the 72-TET 80
Figure 85: Row of *maqam Rast* and its *dauauin*. 81
Figure 86: Row of *maqam Saba* on *D* and its *dauauin*. 82
Figure 87: *Ajnas* in *Jadaka L-Ghaith*. M*aqam Huzam* on *E*. 84
Figure 88: Row of *maqam Huzam* on *E*. 85
Figure 89: Notes from a row *maqam* is used in the Syrian Desert 85
Figure 90: Simplified row *maqam* for the previous example. 85
Figure 91: Possible *ajnas* in the previous simplified row of *maqam* in 24-TET. 86
Figure 92: Row of *maqam Bastah-Nikar*. 86
Figure 93: Row of overtone *maqam* on *C*. 87
Figure 94: *jins* $C_{(11,12,13,15)}$. 91
Figure 95: Possible overtone *ajnas* Sikah in a C.M.O.S. 91
Figure 96: C.M.O.S-*Sikah*. 92
Figure 97: Opera *Qadmoos*, Storyteller Scene (Antara), *maqam Sikah* 92
Figure 98: Row *maqam Sikah*. 92

Figure 99: Overtone *maqam Sikah* on E 93
Figure 100: Hypothetic spectrogram illustration for an accord from the *maqam Sikah* on E spectral from..93
Figure 101: Possible overtone *ajnas* of the C.M.O.S. in the row of *maqam Sikah*. 94
Figure 102: *Qadmoos*, Storyteller Scene (*Antara, The Storyteller Starts His Game*), bars 1-2 94
Figure 103: *Qadmoos*, Storyteller Scene (*Antara*): melody in E M.O.S. 95
Figure 104: Chosen location for sound spectrogram of the Sygyt style solo singing at the "Huun Huur Tu" at the Philadelphia Folk Festival, August 2006..97
Figure 105: Overtone pitches that the singer of the Sygyt style of the Tuvan Khoomei uses in his overtone song written in the 72-TET. 97
Figure 106: Melodies from the analysis of the Sygyt style singer of the Tuvan Khoomei "Huun Huur Tu" at the Philadelphia Folk Festival, August 2006..98
Figure 107: Two tones harmony for *maqam Rast* written in 24-TET. 99
Figure 108: Four tones harmony for the overtone *maqam Rast* rewritten in 72-TET. The fundamentals B and G_{+2cnts} are missing. 99
Figure 109: Four tones harmony for *maqam Rast* written in 24-TET................99
Figure 110: The above *maqam Rast* four tones overtone harmony rewritten in 72-TET. The fundamentals B and G_{+2cnts} are missing. 100
Figure 111: Storyteller Scene, *Antara: The holy war*, bar. 158. A random harmonic movement for an overtone *maqam* within a C M.O.S............101
Figure 112: Parallel harmony movement for three different *qararat* of *maqam Bayati*. 102
Figure 113: *Minus One Beautiful One* for Cello. 104
Figure 114: Part of the piece *Minus One Beautiful One,* in microtonal movements between D, A and F, C..105
Figure 115: Transforming three matrices to musical pitches..............................107
Figure 116: Illustration of *Sudoku* game with the musical background.............108
Figure 117: Illustration of the main nine divisions of the 81-TET *Sudoku* scale 107
Figure 118: Nine principle pitches of *Sudoku*/ 9-TET scale...............................109
Figure 119: Illustration of the first nine divisions of the 81-TET of the *Sudoku* scale..109
Figure 120: The game will not be ruined by switching between lines, but the music will change in a logical way according to the number distributions..110
Figure 121: Alternative matrix reading for *Sudoku*. 110
Figure 122: *Sparkling Stone* for solo five string cello, C, G, D, A, E. 111
Figure 123: *Sparkling Stone* for solo five- string cello. 112
Figure 124: *Barada,* for nine instruments in a blended spectrum. Bar 4 is written in C M.O.S. to be performed randomly. 113

Figure 125: *Barada, maqam* modulations..113
Figure 126: Simplified row of *maqam Mahur* on *C*. 114
Figure 127: Simplified row of *maqam Rast* on *C*. 114
Figure 128: Simplified row of *maqam Sikah* on *E*. 114
Figure 129: Simplified row of *maqam Nairuz*. 114
Figure 130: Simplified row of *maqam Mustaar* on *G*. 114
Figure 131: Row of *maqam Husaini* on *D*...115
Figure 132: *Mesopotamian tears:* polyphonic movement for melodies written in two *ajnas, jins Bayati* on *C* and *jins Rast* on *D*..115
Figure 133: Row of *maqam Husaini* on *D*...116
Figure 134: Overtones from the *D* overtone series are chosen to the nearest tones in *maqam Husaini* putting into consideration, the overtones are written in the 72-TET and the *maqam* is written in the 24-TET............116
Figure 135: From *Qadmoos*, Storyteller scene (*Anrara, The storyteller starts his game*), Bars 33-36. Polyphonic movement of *maqam Husaini* on *D*.........117
Figure 136: *Mesopotamian Tears,* Bars 326-328*: C* Spectrum in harmony and melody. 118
Figure 137: Program performs randomly a melody in a certain M.O.S...........119
Figure 138: Program performs randomly a melody in a certain M.O.S. in different octaves. 119
Figure 139: Program performs randomly a melody in M.O.S. This melody modulates from one M.O.S. to another in different octaves..................120
Figure 140: Program randomly performs a melody in M.O.S. accompanied by a parallel harmonic line in M.O.S 121
Figure 141: Program randomly performs a melody in M.O.S. accompanied by two parallel harmonic lines in M.O.S..122
Figure 142: Strings part of the Overture of *Qadmoos,* Bars. 18-21 demonstrating harmony and melody by using the *D* spectrum 123
Figure 142 b: Woodwind part of the Overture of *Qadmoos,* Bars. 20-26 demonstrating harmony and melody 124
Figure 143: *Qadmoos*, Storyteller Scene (*Antara, The holy war*), Bars.15-16. 125
Figure 144: A M.O.S. 126
Figure 145: A C.M.O.S. 126
Figure 146: Opera *Qadmoos*, Storyteller Scene (*Antara, The holy war*), Bars 15-16. Modulations between two C.M.O.S.: *A* and *Aes*. 126
Figure 147: Storyteller Scene (*Antara, The holy war*), Bars 19-24. Modulation between different tuning systems: C.M.O.S., Chromatic scale and *maqam*. 127
Figure 148: Storyteller Scene (*Antara, The holy war*), Bar 29-31. Modulation (/−|) from B C.M.O.S. to A C.M.O.S.................................128
Figure 149: Chromatic 12-tone scale derived from the C.M.O.S. 129
Figure 150: Overtonal simplified row of *maqam* with new category for the *ajnas*. 129
Figure 151 129

Figure 152: A simplified row of overtonal *maqam* with new category for the *ajnas*. 129

Figure 153: Storyteller Scene (*Antara, The holy war*), Bars 22-24. Modulation for the chromatic overtonal *maqamat* from C to D and then from D to H. 130

Figure 154: *Antara* scene: Modulation to the third M.O.S.:E M.O.S. modulates to H M.O.S. and then to Fis M.O.S 131

Figure 155: E M.O.S. 132

Figure 156: H M.O.S. 132

Figure 157: Spectrogram analysis for a female voice saying "Strong" with 133

Figure 158: A male sound has a normal frequency of 90. 2307 Hz when pronouncing the letter S. 134

Figure 159: A male sound has a normal frequency of 90. 2307 Hz when pronouncing Sh. 134

Figure 160: A male sound has a normal frequency of 90.2307 Hz when pronouncing *Ga*. 135

Figure 161: Storyteller Scene (*Antara, The gang leader's will*), Bars 1-6 136

Samples from Opera Qadmoos, Storyteller scene "Antara"

Qadmoos
Overture

Rami C

The Storyteller enters the Parliament

The Gang Leader and His Brother

The Prince and his Aphrodite

The Victims in the Hands of the Gang Leaders

The First Victim in the Cage

He Loves Him/She

Duel Between the Macho and Aphrodite

The Gang Leader`s Will

The First Victim in the Cage

A Full Instigation

The Holy War

Happy Massacre End

www.ingramcontent.com/pod-product-compliance
Lightning Source LLC
Chambersburg PA
CBHW051614230426
43668CB00013B/2105